T0146408

Beyond
TWO WORLDS

A Taiwanese-American Adoptee's Memoir
& Search for Identity

MARIJANE HUANG

authorHOUSE®

AuthorHouse™
1663 Liberty Drive
Bloomington, IN 47403
www.authorhouse.com
Phone: 1 (800) 839-8640

Published by AuthorHouse   03/29/2017

ISBN: 978-1-5246-8410-5 (sc)
ISBN: 978-1-5246-8408-2 (hc)
ISBN: 978-1-5246-8409-9 (e)

Library of Congress Control Number: 2017904198

Print information available on the last page.

This book is printed on acid-free paper.

To my parents, Wendell and Gloria and to Ma and Pa whose everlasting wish for our family to be reunited one day came true.

There is no greater burden than carrying an untold story inside you.
~ Maya Angelou *(1928-2014)*

Marijane Huang's journey in search of her birth family and her "rediscovery" of newfound cultural roots is one of the most captivating and moving stories you will ever read. When we first featured excerpts of her story as it was unfolding, it instantly became one of the most shared and talked-about articles throughout our community.

In the 2nd generation Taiwanese American community, we are all too familiar with stories of personal struggle as individuals come to terms with their bi-cultural identity and sense of belonging in America. The exploration of our parents' experiences is often the foundation from which the answers to our questions can be found. But, what happens when all of your assumptions about family and identity are turned upside down? The revelations from Huang's adoption story and how she deals with each piece of new and sometimes shocking information sheds important light on how much our past and present relationships, as well as our desire to know from where we come, continue to shape who we are today. It's an excellent reminder that truth and reconciliation are essential in achieving ultimate fulfillment in our lives moving forward.

Beyond Two Worlds is an unforgettable testament to family history through the eyes of an adoptee with a life full of experiences. Marijane Huang's story--both a nail-biting thriller and tearjerker drama... if a personal memoir could ever be described as such--is a must-read for anyone who has ever contemplated the importance of family, lineage, and the strengthened sense of identity they give us through the generations.

— Ho Chie Tsai, Founder of TaiwaneseAmerican.org,
a website highlighting the amazing stories of Taiwanese America

Contents

Acknowledgments 致谢

I wish to thank some very special people who have supported me during the production of this book. First, Carole Ann Kaplan. My dear friend, Carole, was a writing teacher where I attended high school in Louisiana and very popular with the students. I did not take any of her classes, which is most bizarre, because it certainly feels as though I had. Carole managed a writing group on Facebook that I joined in 2010. She encouraged me to create my blog, *Beyond Two Worlds*, and became my biggest fan. Not only has Carole encouraged me to write all these years, but has been with me since the beginning of the search and reunion for my birth family. She graciously read each chapter of this book at every stage from start to finish, offering kind words when I most needed them and insightful feedback. Carole has been the wind beneath my wings, a mentor and confidante and supporter and believer of my work. Carole, I am inspired by your bold and beautiful spirit.

An enormous thanks to my editor, Allyson Sharp, who had the vision for what this book could become. Thank you for challenging me to dig deeper, for your invaluable feedback and insight, and most of all encouragement and support. You are the reason my story will see the light of day.

To Shuchen Chuang, thank you for your timely assistance with translation where needed and for your kind support. I have always appreciated your sunny disposition.

Thanks to Laura McKnight, a dear friend and fellow social worker, who provided a listening ear on countless occasions and lent interminable support while I wrote the pages of this story. Thank you for your interest and reading the early chapters. Thanks, Mr. Jerel Cain, for inspiring me to step out and write about what I am most passionate about. Your encouragement helped spark the creative process. Thanks to Nicole Hogan for your enthusiasm to continue writing this story after reading a very rough couple of first chapters and then connecting me to Allyson, our mutual editor. Thanks to all who have followed, and who continue to follow my blog, *Beyond Two Worlds (https://beyondtwoworlds.com/)* - adoptees, adoptive parents, and friends. Without you, I would never have dared to write this book.

A loving thanks to my husband, Pat, who patiently endured hours of my sitting in front of a computer to finish this story. And to my daughter, Lexie, you are the light of my life. I hope this story inspires you as you have inspired me.

Finally, thanks to Christina and Amy, my dear sisters, who embraced me as their little sister, *mèi mei,*没没, after nearly forty years of separation and have never let go. You inspire me and are role-models of everything lovely and noble.

Author's Note 作者的按语

People often say this or that person has not yet found himself. But the self is not something that one finds. It is something that one creates. ~ Thomas Szasz

It brings me unbelievable joy and gratitude to share this unique journey with you. In sharing my story, I hope to provide support and encouragement to others seeking a connection with their birth family. For years, I have thought about writing this memoir encouraged by friends, but had difficulty wrapping my mind around how to tell such a labyrinthine story. After much thought, prayer, and most especially, other adoptees, I was drawn to put all the pieces together as though the force of gravity itself were pulling me toward my past. One inspired morning, I sat down at my computer to tell the story of how one forty-two year-old adoptee began searching across the world for her birth family.

To search for one's birth family on the other side of the ocean is a quest that is quite daunting. There is, of course, the investigative piece, navigating through language barriers and government agencies, searching for documents and the right people who are willing and able to help. According to the U.S. Department of State, there were 261,728 international or inter-country adoptions worldwide from 1999 to 2015 (U.S. Department of State, 2016). International adoptions to the U.S. peaked in 2004 at 22,989; however, there has been a sharp decline in such adoptions due primarily to stricter international adoption laws enacted to banish child trafficking and unethical international adoption practices. (U.S. Department of State, 2016). In fiscal year 2015, there were 5,648 international adoptions to the U.S. (U.S. Department of State, 2016). International adoption continues to decline as countries attempt to place orphaned children domestically first before considering adoptive families from other countries.

The process of searching for one's birth family is often amplified by the emotional and psychological consequences that affect many adoptees as a result of multiple losses, the most significant being the loss of the adoptee's birth mother, but also that of a culture, language, and original family. Nancy Newton Verrier aptly defines this loss as the primal wound. In her book of the same name, Verrier speaks of the bonding in utero of mother and child. She cites the research of pediatrician, T.B. Brazelton, whose pioneering research on child development and clinical practice led to the establishment of the Brazelton Institute of Boston Children's Hospital. Verrier (1993) explains,

> *Many doctors and psychologists now understand that bonding doesn't begin at birth, but is a continuum of physiological, psychological, and spiritual events, which begin in utero and continue throughout the postnatal bonding period. When this natural evolution is interrupted by a postnatal separation from the biological mother, the resultant experience of abandonment and loss is indelibly imprinted upon the unconscious minds of these children, causing that which I call the "primal wound (p.1)."*

Verrier (1993) likens an adoptee's relinquishment to that of *"a kind of death, not only of the mother, but of part of the Self, that core-being or essence of oneself which makes one feel whole"* (p.6). She continues,

> *In acknowledging this loss and its impact on all involved in adoption, there is no way one can get around the pain: the pain of separation and loss for both the child and the birthmother, and the pain of not understanding or being able to make up for that pain and loss on the part of the adoptive parents* (p.6).

In many cases, when a family seeks therapy to address behavioral or emotional issues displayed by an adopted child treatment focuses on the relationship between the child and adoptive parents without consideration to the impact of the initial trauma on the child and, subsequently, adoptive family (Verrier, 1993). Additionally, international and transracial adoptees must navigate through two different cultures. Assimilation into the predominant culture is frequently not a seamless process.

In my own life, the primal wound manifested itself as fear, anxiety, and feelings of not belonging. From as far back as I can remember I experienced an intense feeling of differentness, of never fitting in with those around me. I felt detached from my peers and adults alike, and there was no explanation for it. Some mistakenly labeled me as aloof, but in reality, I lacked the ability to communicate with others. I was painfully shy and had difficulty making and retaining friends, which only exacerbated those feelings. It was quite isolating and went deeper than mere physical differences in appearance from my family and peers. I can only describe it as a feeling of being lost, a lonely ache that never dulled, although I could never quite put a finger to it or verbalize such feelings until much later in my life. I also suffered from extreme separation anxiety as a young child. I was the youngster who screamed inconsolably whenever my mother left me at the nursery. I had nightmares and startled easily at loud noises, especially thunder, which scared me half out of my wits. I covered my ears and cowered in fear at the hint of a thunderstorm. My father, who was once a pilot in the USAF, took me every year to see the Thunderbirds perform at Barksdale Air Force Base. I hunkered beneath the car seat and held my hands tightly over my ears, longing for the show to come to an abrupt end. In elementary school, I experienced unbearable stomach pains and complained almost daily to my teacher, Ms. Dent. I begged her to call my mother to pick me up from school each time these incidents occurred. One morning, I caught Ms. Dent whispering to the other teachers apprehensively, wondering what to do with me. On one such occasion, my mother left work to pick me up from school only to take me home and promptly spank me for causing such trouble. She yelled and I cried, not understanding why she should punish me for feeling sick to my stomach. My mother did not know how acutely I felt the pain of separation and the anxiety it caused me. As a young adult, I learned to adjust and overcome the "differentness" by using alcohol and drugs. Much later, I became a Christian, and my faith in God helped me overcome some of those old insecurities; my husband, Pat, and my daughter, Lexie, along with my formal education in social work also assisted in providing refuge. However, it would be years more before I would find my own voice and feel comfortable in my own skin. I spent many years confused about who I was, trying desperately to "fit in" and could not explain how and why I felt as I did. Though some may argue against it, I am certain now that it all began with the primal wound.

I never wished to connect with my birth culture or family while growing up or well into my adulthood. In fact, I did everything I could to minimize my Asian appearance and at my core, felt just as white as everyone around me. I self-identified as White, not Asian; however, certain significant events fortuitously changed that. The desire to connect to my birth heritage eventually took root and became undeniable. The curiosity and wonder behind where I came from, the relinquishment and unknowns became a driving force. It is this personal experience, a maturation that changed me from the inside out, that is highlighted in this narrative. I cannot begin to express how much my perspective as an adoptee has evolved regarding my adoption and that of international adoption. I want to emphasize that this story is deeply personal and unique to my own life and experiences. I dare not speak for other adoptees, although I often find common ground with them. To the best of my knowledge and recounts, I have captured experiences from my adoption, the search for my birth family, and the rollercoaster of emotions from this incredible journey. It is a story told as I remember it. To protect the privacy of those impacted by my story, some names have been changed, as adoption uncovers many skeletons, and some wish to remain buried.

My search took years and was inevitably difficult due to multiple barriers. Fortunately, my parents signed and received a contract of adoption from the agency where they adopted me. They carefully preserved this document, and it later became the precipice of my search. During the years that it took to finally reach my birth family, my hope waned more times than I can remember. There were long lapses in communication despite the gallant efforts of my brave social worker. As providence would have it, reunion finally occurred, but only after much persistence and patience. So, for those seeking answers, do not give up. Trust that in the end, your journey will take you where you are meant to be. It is with these words I present my story of love, despair, joy, isolation, and reconnection to a birth culture that had long been forsaken.

发现

Discover

1.

Some beautiful paths can't be discovered without getting lost.
~ Erol Ozan

Imagine your whole life believing that you are one thing and then learning in mid-life that you are not what you have always believed you were. Let me explain. When I was four months old, I was adopted in Taipei, Taiwan by a white American military family. My dad, Wendell Buck, was a lieutenant colonel in the United States Air Force, and he and my mom, Gloria, were stationed in Okinawa. Both of my parents were in their early forties at the time of my adoption in December of 1966. They shared very little about my adoption, and I knew even less about my birth family and heritage. I did not come to know or understand the terms, "birth family," "biological family," "birth culture," until much later in my life. Growing up, I told others that I was Japanese and Vietnamese. That is what my adoptive parents told me, that is what I believed. I had no reason to question what I had been told. Why would I? After my mother passed away in 2008, however, I made a discovery about my adoption and origins that changed the course of my life forever.

Mom was diagnosed with Alzheimer's disease some years after Dad passed away from a massive heart attack in January, 1993. To observe Mom deteriorate slowly over the years into a phantom of the woman she was during her most vibrant years was most cruel. She suffered from Alzheimer's for nearly twelve years before finally succumbing on February 29, 2008, Leap Day. As a young woman, Mom was slender and of average height. She was quite fashionable and wore her shoulder length brown hair set in waves, as was the style in the 1930's and forties. Mom was a Registered Nurse and worked full-time as the Director of Nursing at multiple skilled nursing homes across the years. She typically came home from work exhausted, but no matter how tired she was, there was a home-cooked meal on the table at six o'clock every evening.

Dad was a meat and potatoes kind of guy, so dinner was typically something like meat loaf, or fried chicken with potatoes, green beans fried in bacon grease, and always an ice-burg salad. Mom baked a mouth-watering homemade apple and pecan pie and used Crisco like it was going out of style. But, Mom's pièce de résistance was her fried rice. Oh, how we loved Mom's fried rice! To this day, I cannot replicate her recipe, hard as I try. There was something about just the right shake of Kikkoman and pinch of ginger that made Mom's fried rice special. Fridays, we went out to dinner, and Pancho's Mexican Buffet was one of our favorite restaurants. Hungry diners were offered the typical Mexican-American faire served buffet-style. Servers slopped soft enchiladas oozing with green or red sauce and refried beans and rice onto warm, stainless steel platters. My favorite was always the Sopapillas. I drenched the puffy, fried pastries with butter and honey, the sticky goodness dripping off my fingers.

* * *

My parents married on October 6, 1962, in Omaha, Nebraska where Dad was stationed at Offut Air Force Base. On February 25, 1963, just four short months after their wedding, Dad suffered a cerebral hemorrhage, which nearly took his life. Mom said he was at home using his exercise bike and began complaining of a horrible headache when he suddenly became incapacitated. Dad told me his younger sister, Dorothy, died of the same condition at a much younger age. Mom accompanied Dad via emergency air evacuation on a T-29 military aircraft to San Antonio, Texas where he underwent immediate surgery. He was not expected to survive. I imagine Mom was sick with worry. One day, I found the original Western Union telegram that was wired to Dad's mother, who lived in California, describing his fragile condition.

Dad was a bit of a pack rat, and the telegram lay at the bottom of an old cigar box beneath old pens and other miscellaneous junk. It read,

1963 FEB 26 PM 7 01

I WISH TO OFFICIALLY INFORM YOU THAT YOUR SON MAJOR WENDELL R BUCK, 37033A, WAS PLACED ON THE SERIOUSLY ILL LIST AT THE 865 USAF HOSPITAL, OFFUTT, AFB, NEBRASKA, AT 1200 HOURS ON 26 FEBRUARY 1963, AS A RESULT OF A CEREBRAL HEMORRHAGE. HIS RECOVERY IS QUESTIONABLE. HE IS BEING EVACUATED BY AIRCRAFT TO THE USAF HOSPITAL LACKLAND AFB, SAN ANTONIO, TEXAS, IMMEDIATELY. THE ATTENDING PHYSICAN RECOMMENDS YOUR IMMEDIATE PRESENCE AT HIS BEDSIDE. IN THE EVENT YOU ARE UNABLE TO VISIT HIM AT LACKLAND AFB, THE HOSPITAL COMMANDER WILL FURNISH YOU A REPORT ON HIS CONDITION EVERY FIVE DAYS, UNLESS A SIGNIFICANT CHANGE OCCURS IN WHICH CASE THEY WILL ADVISE YOU IMMEDIATELY. PLEASE ACCEPT MY SINCERE SYMPATHY IN THIS TIME OF ANXIETY=

ELKINS READ JR COLONEL USAF COMMANDER==

I do not know if Dad's mother was able to visit him at Lackland AFB in Texas, or if Mom communicated with her very often after they were married. We visited Dad's mother when I was a very young girl once, but I do not remember much of that visit, except that we drove out to California to see her. It was dark as we traveled to her home, and when I looked out the car window, I could see the moonlight reflected off the black waves of the ocean. In one of Mom's old diaries, I found an entry that followed Dad's surgery. Mom wrote faithfully, year after year, in her diaries entrusting some of her most intimate concerns to those pages. She wrote:

> *"Wendy operated on. Subarachnoid brain hemorrhage.*
> *God spared his life. Thank you dear Lord."*

I could hear the depth of relief in Mom's words, though brief, as though she had just received the best news of her life. Dad spent months in rehabilitation to strengthen and regain the use of his left side. He was left partially paralyzed and experienced excruciating headaches following his surgery. Dad learned to walk again and complete the activities of daily living, like tying his shoelaces, things he once took for granted. Mom did not write further about Dad's recovery in her diary, but Dad told me the sound of her pantyhose as she walked across his hospital room was tormenting.

Two months following this harrowing event in my parent's lives, Mom began practical nursing training at the Omaha Public School, Vocational Education Department in Practical Nursing. She graduated in April, 1964, and successfully passed her state boards. Years later, Mom, at the age of forty-seven, returned to school to become a Registered Nurse. Classes were held at a satellite campus of Northwestern University on the campus of Louisiana State University in Shreveport, Louisiana. Occasionally, Mom took me to class with her during the summer months, no doubt when she was unable to find a babysitter. I would sit quietly in the back of class, half bored out of my little mind.

For two long years, Mom struggled through nursing school, juggling the demands of a full-time nursing job and studying late nights. I never saw Mom studying, but in her diary, I learned that she often studied biology, anatomy, chemistry, and psychology after my niece, Katy, and I were in bed for the night. She was anguished by the difficulty of her biology labs and severely disappointed after failing some of her tests. Mom never gave up though and eventually graduated in August, 1974. The image of Mom wearing her stark white nursing uniform, white stockings and shoes, and a nursing cap upon her coiffed short brown hair reminds me of what a tenacious woman she was and her deep passion for nursing.

Once her career as an RN was established, Mom worked tirelessly. She sometimes took me to work with her. On one occasion, there was an Easter egg hunt at the nursing home. Residents shuffled into the lobby with their canes and walkers and were partnered with nursing aides, most of them African American. The linoleum white floors were dull, and the smell of urine clung to the air. At Mom's urging, I reluctantly grabbed hold of the hand of a heavy-set African American woman, her affect was as flat as stone, her other hand held tight to a colorful straw basket. She limped along as I held her hand. I looked up at her stony face, but she stared straight ahead, never once speaking to me. We searched the yard together, silently looking for eggs. I felt awkward holding onto this woman's hand, unsure what to say or what to do. Nevertheless, it made Mom happy that I was there participating with the residents and staff she so dearly loved.

* * *

I am not certain how my parents first met. They did not divulge much, so I have always wondered. Both of my parents were married previously, and Mom's first husband was also in the U.S. Army Air Corp. Mom and Dad had teenaged children from their first marriages when they finally adopted me, but I have no recollection of them at this early stage in my life. Dad had a long, respected career in the U.S. Air Force. He was a pilot and flew B-29's, B-47's, and B-52's until the hemorrhage interrupted his career. He was a quiet man, yet had a contagious sense of humor and a gentle smile. He often brought home jokes to share with my mom that made us all laugh, except for the ones that were for adults only. He was quite handsome as a young man, about six feet tall with a slender build, and the kind of wavy blond hair that made the ladies swoon.

Dad began his military career at the young age of eighteen years old, drafted by the U.S. Army Air Corp and served in the Second World War. He became a pilot and then served as co-pilot aboard a B-24 Liberator called Rebel Gal. After the war, he flew C-54's with the Allied forces in the Berlin Airlift ferrying provisions from Western Europe to Germany and was stationed at Weisbaden. He never talked about his exploits during the war. I often asked Dad when I was a little girl if he ever got shot. *"No,"* he would say. *"Shot at."* And that was the end of the conversation.

Unfortunately, Dad was disqualified from ever flying again after he suffered the cerebral hemorrhage due to physical impairment. I am sure this crushed him. The home I was raised in was decorated from wall to wall with his military accolades, telling a story I never knew or much appreciated as a child. Dad was eventually reassigned to Director of Personnel, a position he kept for the remainder of his military career and transfers. I have often wondered if he and Mom would have adopted me had he not suffered the hemorrhage because his career as a pilot in the USAF was so successful.

Dad finally retired at Barksdale Air Force Base in Bossier City, Louisiana after twenty-nine years of devoted service. His retirement ceremony on the base was quite a formality. The sound of my feet traipsing up the metal bleachers sounded hollow to my young ears as Mom held tightly to my small hand. What I remember most about that ceremony was the military guard in full regalia carrying the American and military flags round about. Their crisp, navy blue uniforms, colorful medals, and white gloves spoke loudly of honor and service. The guard stopped and gave Dad a full salute as they passed him by, and Dad returned their salute stiffly. I am certain Dad was regretful that his military career had to end. It was a way a life for him and Mom for many years. Dad had difficulty at first seeking work as a civilian. He held many odd jobs and was a gas station attendant for a time, then a real estate agent before going back to college to pursue his B.A. Like Mom, he was in his late forties when he went back to school. After graduating from Louisiana Tech, Dad landed a job with the State of Louisiana inspecting water. He sometimes brought home samples of nasty, polluted-looking water in transparent containers, no doubt in need of testing. Eventually, this led to a higher paying position as a Transportation Inspector inspecting eighteen-wheelers out at what he called "the scales." He woke up at the same time every morning to the sound of his alarm, put on his brown and tan uniform, carefully attaching his gold name badge to his shirt before having a cup or two of joe. The little white building where he worked was situated in Pinewood, Louisiana right at the Louisiana and Texas state borders. Dad worked this job right up until the day he died on January 23rd, 1993.

When my dad retired, we moved off the military base at Barksdale and settled in a little suburb of Bossier City. Bossier City is a rural city located along the east bank of the Red River across from Shreveport in the Northwest region of Louisiana. When the rains came during the winter months, the belly of the Red River swelled, spilling over the hard red-clay banks and flooding lowland communities. We once took a trip in my parent's old aqua Chrysler right under the Jimmy Davis Bridge on the other side of Shreveport to the river banks and collected sand for my plastic, sea turtle sandbox. *"Careful,"* Mom cautioned me as I skipped from one sand bank to the next. We got plenty of sand that day and rushed home where my sandbox waited to be filled.

The neighborhood I grew up in was a mostly white middle-class community where several military families lived. All the streets were named after planets, and ours so happened to be Pluto Drive. The neighbors knew each other, and the kids on the block became my friends, although we did not share the same classes in school. We stayed out late playing red rover, red rover, or red light green light on our grassy lawn until our parents called us into dinner, the magenta skies bidding us farewell until the next evening.

As a child, I felt safe growing up in our home, our neighborhood. Single-family brick homes lined the streets and, the lawns were green and carefully manicured. Some families had pools in their backyard, as did ours. The morning they began building our pool, I was filled with anticipation and peered out my bedroom window excitedly, jumping up and down on my bed. The sound of drills and machinery went on for days until one day we had a brand new sparkling pool waiting to be plunged into. I clung to the walls of that pool for dear life until Mom promptly enrolled me in swim lessons at the local YMCA. During the summer months when torrential rainstorms wreaked havoc, Dad was forced to drain the excess water out of the pool. After the rains, all the kids loved playing in the ditch just behind our home, which I was strictly forbidden to do. The rain filled the ditch till it was brimming with dirty brown water, and we gathered old Tupperware containers to catch tiny minnows or crawdads, scooping them up with glee. One day, Dad caught me walking home from school along the ditch. I thought I had been so careful sneaking behind the ditch and hiding behind overgrown shrubs, but was filled with guilt. When I got home, Dad was waiting, and I was promptly spanked for disobeying.

Mine was a spoiled childhood. I had no want for anything. It would not be until I reached adolescence that this idyllic upbringing would drastically change, and what was once a safe and comfortable childhood would evolve into unrelenting conflict between my parents and I, not unlike what other teens experience. Yet racial teasing coupled with my own deep insecurity caused an identity crisis and such confusion that further complicated the relationship between my parents and I, leaving an indelible mark upon my psyche that would take years to heal.

* * *

Mom had entered the last stages of Alzheimer's disease by 2006. It was unbearable to see the drastic changes in her physical appearance. She lay in a hospital bed at home, her eyes stared into nothingness, her mouth gaped open, her body weakened and emaciated. Her arms jerked uncontrollably at times, and she struggled with seizures. When I visited, which was typically only once a year for about a week, I sat beside Mom, holding her hand, staring at her hollowed out face. I was racked with guilt and angry that I was unable to visit more frequently due to our lack of finances.

Before Mom passed, my half sister, Margaret, began rummaging through our parents' attic in an attempt to get rid of junk. Margaret was Mom's primary caregiver with the assistance of hospice. She was tall with freckles and long, bleached blond hair. She had a southern accent as thick as molasses and had always been slender. We had discussed moving Mom to California at an earlier stage of the disease so that I could care for her, but Mom did not want to leave her home where she felt safe and comfortable. Margaret was eleven years older than I and had not always been the best role model. She got pregnant at the age of eighteen and eventually married the father of her first child, Katy, although the marriage ended in divorce. My parents practically raised Katy, and she and I grew up together for some years before she decided to live permanently with her mom and step-father, Rick, Margaret's second husband. Katy was feisty and had a much more colorful personality in comparison to my quiet and introverted character. Margaret and Rick moved in with us when I was in high school. When they moved in, I moved to the smaller bedroom right next to theirs. One day, I found large bags full of a gazillion pills, little pink hearts and white ones with blue speckles, in the bedroom they occupied, which at one time, was my bedroom. I often wondered if Mom and Dad knew about all their shenanigans, but since nothing changed, I guessed they did not. My parents kept out of my sister and Rick's business for the most part.

I imagined my sister prior to Mom's death foraging her way through that old dank attic thick with nasty cobwebs and ancient mousetraps. There were tons of boxes taped up from top to bottom, and none of us had a clue as to their contents. Why had Mom and Dad never rid themselves of all that junk? I was glad Margaret was willing to brave her way through the attic. We were quite fortunate she did because one of the boxes, we were later to learn, held some very surprising things that changed my life profoundly.

* * *

My husband, Pat, and daughter, Lexie, traveled back to Louisiana with me for Mom's funeral. That morning, it was chilly, but the sun shone brightly and brilliant white clouds floated high in the sky, impervious to the grief that bore down upon me. Pat and Lexie got ready in silence. Lexie was only ten years old at the time. I was lost in my own thoughts and sadness. Mom survived fifteen years following my dad's death, which nearly broke her heart. Thank goodness Grandma Bushmiller, my mother's mom, lived with her; otherwise, I think Mom would surely have fallen apart. Grandma Bushmiller was Mom's companion all those lonely years after Dad died. I struggled with guilt that morning over not having been more present during the years Mom was sick. My family and I lived in California, and it was difficult to get back to visit due to work, finances, and other obligations.

I had a tumultuous relationship with my mom, and I realized that we had never talked about how awful we were to each other. I never sought her forgiveness nor did Mom ever ask for mine. There was so much left unsaid, unfinished, and once Mom had Alzheimer's, it was too late. Years passed, and although I talked to Mom regularly on the phone, I would return home one day and find that she no longer recognized me. I could not believe it. She had declined drastically, and it was a shock. All those phone conversations we had led me to believe she knew whom she was speaking to; but that was not the case.

On one particular visit back home to Louisiana, I stopped by Mom's after dinnertime. She was still ambulatory, yet confused and needed supervision at all times. She had reached the mid-stages of the disease process. I had flown in from California without Pat and Lexie a couple of days earlier and had been visiting Mom daily. I never stayed in our home when I visited because it had become so run down and smelled badly of smoke and pet urine. The carpets were old and threadbare, the walls stained from cigarette smoke, and the house had become cluttered with junk over the years. My sister, Margaret, was typically around, but that evening, she went out. I walked through the door, and when Mom saw me, she immediately ran towards me, her eyes frantic. *"What happened? Why did I leave you?"* she said to me on the verge of tears. She searched my face intently, grabbing my hands, confused.

"Oh, Mom! You didn't leave me. It's me, Marijane, your adopted daughter," I tried to explain. "You and Dad adopted me. Do you remember?" Of course she did not remember, and I knew better than to ask. But, I did not know how to help her or what to say. I could see the confusion behind her eyes as she tried desperately to remember who I was. All I could do was hold her frail, withered hands and smile, reassuring her that everything was okay. I believed there was a flicker of recognition, but she could not put all the pieces together. That night I sat on the couch close to Mom holding her hands, and we cried. She would often turn to look at my face and smile, her eyes searching, bewildered. My heart ached. I did not want that evening to end because I knew, once I left, she would not remember. I stayed as long as I could then cried all the way back to my hotel. The next morning, the previous evening had vanished from Mom's memory, lost forever within the tangled recesses of her mind.

Years later at my mom's funeral, the service was brief. It was difficult to tear myself away from Mom's graveside, just as it was at my father's funeral. I stood there beneath the dark green canopy erected by funeral services, waiting for some sign that it was time to go. It never came. My eyes were puffy and red from crying, and the tissue I held in my hand had shriveled into tiny, torn pieces.

After the funeral, Margaret, my niece, Katy, and my nephew, Kyle, and I went to eat at Strawn's Eat Shop with a close family friend, Mrs. Reynolds, who had come to the funeral from Monroe, Louisiana where she lived. Pat and Lexie were also with us. Mrs. Reynolds, her daughter,

Mandi, and her two sons, Fred and Chuck, were our next-door neighbors when I was a kid. Mrs. Reynolds taught nursing at Grambling University and was one of Mom's closest friends. She had instructed some of Mom's classes at Northwestern University in Shreveport. Mandi was also a Registered Nurse like her mom and my playmate growing up.

Strawn's was a welcome distraction from all the sorrow. It was also an historical monument in Shreveport known for its southern comfort food. I am sure our party was a sight to behold that afternoon - an Asian family lunching with a bunch of white folks, a rarity in those parts. We ate southern fried chicken, biscuits, and Strawn's famous strawberry pie. Delicious, sweet strawberry filling seeped out beneath a generous layer of homemade whipped cream and tickled my taste buds. There were some things about the south that I missed. Memories came flooding back of much happier times. Mrs. Reynolds often came to our home on the weekends to play Bridge with my parents, and there were plenty of martinis for the adults.

Right after Mom's funeral, my family and I headed back to Mom's home with Margaret. After Mom passed, Margaret continued to live in the home for about a year before it was sold. The foul smell of cigarette smoke hit me at once as we walked through the garage door and into the house. I always hated that my parents smoked and that my clothes wreaked of it whenever I went back home. Sometimes the smoke was so thick, I could barely catch my breath. I was the only one in my family in Louisiana who did not smoke.

I began to sort through the boxes that Margaret had brought down from the attic. They sat drearily upon the small dining room table and linoleum floor next to the kitchen and smelled of must. I opened each box precariously unsure of what lay inside. There were items Dad kept from World War Two, things that I assumed were very meaningful to him at one time, like old photos from his youth, flight records, and objects related to his military past. I opened box after box until my fingers were filthy from layers of dust and cobwebs.

After opening the umpteenth box, I stumbled upon something that immediately grabbed my attention. I lifted out a delicate tri-folded document from the box and held it up to the light. The document was yellowed with age and tattered around the edges. As I slowly opened it, my breath caught. The words, CONTRACT OF ADOPTION, were neatly typed across the top of the first page. Was it my original adoption contract? I never knew one existed!

"What is it?" Pat asked.

"Oh, my gosh!" I said. "I think it's my original adoption contract," I replied. I showed the document to Pat, and we studied it. The name, "The Family Planning Association of China," was typed across the page in bold font and was apparently the orphanage in Taipei, Taiwan where I was adopted. The contract was signed by Tze-kuan Shu Kan, Secretary General. She must have been the director of the orphanage. My eyes traced the handwritten signatures of my parents. I recognized Dad's handwriting immediately. There were other articles buried deep inside the box, treasures that surely had some account. The most curious thing of all was a single square picture of my adoptive mom holding me in her lap in what appeared to be an orphanage, although I could not be certain. A small baby bed, its railings rusted and worn, was situated just behind us. The curl of my mother's lips spoke "look what I found." I was unable to take my eyes off the photograph as though bewitched.

I sifted through the remaining articles in the box. I found safety pins that had probably held together my cloth diapers, baby shower cards congratulating my mother on her new addition to the family, and miscellaneous notes, receipts, and letters. I was incredulous.

"Well I'll be damned!" Margaret said peering over my shoulder. "Just look at all that stuff."

"I know. I can't believe it!" I replied. "Did you know anything about these things?" I asked my sister.

"Nope. I don't remember seeing any of this stuff, and Mom never talked about 'em either," Lynn replied.

I looked at my adoption contract again, intrigued by what looked like Mandarin characters neatly written across the pages in vertical fashion. The paper was brittle, and I tried to turn them as gently as possible.

"These must be the names of my birth parents!" I said excitedly to Pat and Margaret, pointing to the contract. There were two different names, Shiow-Jean Lu and Chan-Huai Huang, both written in English.

"It doesn't look like these names are Japanese or Vietnamese. Hmm. That's weird."

"Yeah. What do you know?" replied Margaret with some interest.

"They're definitely not Vietnamese or Japanese," said Pat. My husband would know because he was himself half Vietnamese and Japanese.

I did not understand. Were my birth parents Chinese? Taiwanese? What did that make me? I had always believed myself to be Japanese and Vietnamese as my parents had told me. Questions filled my mind like rapid fire as I contemplated these finds and why my parents kept them from me. I had finally found some tangible link to my adoption. I was baffled by my parent's secrecy. Did they feel threatened that I might search for my birth family? Did they intend to give the items to me, yet never found the appropriate time? It was up to me to figure it all out, and that is exactly what I intended to do.

After finding my adoption contract, I became obsessed with learning about my past. The contract had remained in my parent's attic for nearly forty years as though sequestered. It took a while to let it all sink in – the fact that I was quite possibly not Vietnamese and Japanese. It was almost absurd. A rush of something I had never felt before stirred inside me, like some new high, increasing with each passing day. It was not anger. It was a deep curiosity, an obsession with my cultural roots and a longing to connect. At forty-two years of age, and for the first time in my life, I questioned my parent's story about my adoption. I wondered about my birth parents and the heritage that I had vehemently rejected. Where would these extraordinary finds lead me? What would they eventually reveal? A mysterious door seemed to loom before me like magic. What would I find on the other side? I did not know, but was more than willing to take a chance and find out.

事实

Truth

2.

Then you will know the truth, and the truth will set you free.
~ John 8:32

I do not recall the exact moment when I realized I was adopted. My parents must have told me at a very young age because I just always knew. They often told me that I was "chosen," "special," and Mom occasionally retold the story of how that came to be. Most of the time, she ended up in tears, and I would try my best not to cry in front of her out of embarrassment. Mom would say something like, *"We first saw you in an orange crate. We were shown two babies and did not know which one would be given to us. You smiled, and from that moment, you were the one we wished for."* Mom would typically tell this story after a few martinis, so the accuracy of her story was always a little questionable.

Mom claimed that I was the eleventh child relinquished by my birth parents, and all the girls were placed for adoption. My birthfather was supposedly Japanese and mother, Vietnamese. Mom said they attempted to find one of my biological sisters in Taipei with the hope of adopting her too, but were unsuccessful. Curiously, I found scribbled on pieces of tablet paper a list of several orphanages in the old box. The writing was quite faded and appeared to be in Mandarin, but had English translations. Were these the orphanages my parents visited to look for my sister, or maybe me before finding The Family Planning Association of China?

I was puzzled by my mom's story. So many pieces just did not seem to fit. When I compared her story to the information presented on my adoption contract, clearly much was amiss. In black and white, the contract stated that I was the fourth daughter born to my birth parents, not the eleventh. My birth name was Hsiao-ling Huang. I felt a flood of excitement as I saw my birth name for the very first time. I did not even know how to pronounce it. My parents gave me the middle name, Chaling. I wondered if they changed Hsiao-ling to Chaling. What were they thinking? Why would my parents change the spelling of my birth name? Were they attempting to "Americanize" it? It seemed as though one question led to three more. I wondered if my birth parents and biological siblings were still living? Were they in Taiwan? There was one particular question that burned in my mind. Why was there such a huge discrepancy between Mom's story and my adoption contract? What was the real story? Did the translation get mixed up, or was my mother's story all fabricated? It was hard for me to believe that my parents purposely lied to me, but the discrepancies were blatant. Perhaps the director of the orphanage lied to my parents to influence their decision to adopt me. There was so much I did not know or understand. A memory suddenly popped into my mind while I was thinking through all of this. I remembered a time in college when I asked Mom about my adoption papers, not certain if any existed. I was home visiting from college. Mom sat on the edge of her bed folding clothes.

"Mom, do I have any adoption papers?" I asked quite out of the blue.

"Why do you want to know?" She replied, her eyes narrowed in suspicion. "Who put you up to this?"

I was shocked by her response. "No one, Mom!" I was just asking. "Geez." That familiar look she got when angry caused me to drop the matter like a hot potato. I never thought about my adoption papers again. It was just not that important to me at the time, and I did not want to cause Mom to get more upset. She was quick to become angry, so I tried to avoid that at all costs.

In our household, we walked on eggshells around Mom when she was in one of her moods, which occurred frequently. The minute I sensed a rampage coming on, I retreated to my bedroom and withdrew into myself, hoping and praying that her wrath would not turn on me. I often tried to make Mom smile by making a joke or light of something just to distract her from getting upset. Sometimes it worked. She had a terrible temper and would go off on tirades that lasted hours. Her anger worsened as I got older and wanted more independence and to fit in with my peers. I am sure that some of the conflict arose from the huge generation gap that existed between us. My parents were in their early forties at the time of my adoption and were raised during the Great Depression. They lived through two World Wars in addition to the Korean and Vietnam Wars. Parents during their generation were the authority, and children were to obey without fail. Moreover, they were terribly ill equipped to raise an adopted child of a different race. In the era that I was adopted, adoptive parents were encouraged to assimilate their adopted child to the predominant culture, never to talk about her cultural heritage, and that is exactly what my parents did. I was raised white. Discussions about birth culture and birth families were nonexistent, and there were no trainings available to educate parents on cultural sensitivity or how to integrate an adoptee's cultural heritage into his or her life. Essentially, all ties to my birth heritage were severed. Except, I did not exactly look like my family or peers in the mostly white community I grew up in. I was different. I stuck out like a sore thumb. As a result, I was often teased or ousted by my peers because of my appearance. It did not help that I was incredibly shy and had a hard time making friends at school.

I hated school. From the time I started kindergarten until the end of high school, every school day was a struggle. I did not connect well with my teachers or the other kids, and there were some teachers who treated me differently than my peers, mostly white male teachers. One teacher in particular, a coach, always seemed to yell at me during gym class. I felt demeaned and thought his dislike of me was a result of my shyness and poor athletic ability. It became easier in high school, and I made friends with a couple of girls who I eventually grew close to and trusted, but not before chasing after the popular girls and trying to fit into their circle. They were white, pretty, and sought after by all the guys. Even when I hung out with them, I felt disconnected and reminded of how different I looked from them. I finally realized that it was better to have friends who I could be myself around without booze than to fit in with the popular crowd.

Elementary and middle school were the worst. One day at Sun City Elementary during recess, a crowd of little white boys had gathered around a small area of the playground. I went over to see what all the fuss was about, and there squatting on the ground, was a little Asian boy holding a long, slender stick. He was a new student at the school. The boy was wearing navy blue shorts and a plaid wool vest with a white button-down shirt underneath, not the kind of clothing the other kids wore. His back was turned away from the others, and he sat silently drawing in the dirt with the stick. His face looked sad and defiant at the same time as he attempted to ignore the boys. *"Hey little Chink!"* they taunted and sang in a sing-songy way, pulling up the corners of their eyes. I felt sorry for the boy having experienced similar taunts and walked over to him after the other boys tired of their game.

"Hi," I said kneeling next to him. "My name is Marijane. What's yours?" I wanted to be nice to the boy. After all, we were the only Asians at our school. The little boy ignored me and continued to draw in the dirt. "Are you new here?" I asked. The next thing I knew, I was doubled over in pain, barely able to breathe. The little Asian boy had sucker punched me right in the gut. I limped away from him, hurt and embarrassed, hoping that no one else saw what happened. Soon after, the Asian boy disappeared from school. I do not know exactly what happened. Perhaps the teachers recognized that the little boy was having difficulty fitting in and was being unmercifully teased. I imagined his parents withdrew him as a result, and who could blame them?

The separateness I felt from my peers became deeply rooted and colored my entire world. I felt isolated, an outsider within. Essentially, I wanted to be white, just like every other kid and did everything I could to minimize my Asian appearance. I never shared with my parents that I was teased at school or in the community, nor did they ever ask. It all became part of the conflict that grew between my mom and me. I wanted desperately to fit in with my peers. I wanted more freedom as I aged, yet my mom was very controlling and dictated what I could and could not do, what clubs I could join and activities I could engage in. I despised her because of it and eventually rebelled.

To make matters even worse, Mom was a heavy drinker. She and Dad had a martini or two or three, sometimes more, nightly after work.

Dad came home every evening and mixed up a little pitcher of martinis. Bottles of gin, vodka, vermouth and other hard liquors were readily stored in one of the kitchen cabinets. My niece, Katy, and I would steal the green olives from my parent's martini glasses when we were little girls. The taste of the bitter alcohol on the olives made my lips pucker. It was all very cute until I grew up and understood that Mom and Dad drank too much.

One night in high school, I brought a boyfriend home, and Mom had had a few too many. She sloshed her words as I introduced her to my boyfriend and carried on in such a way that was embarrassing. I was mortified. It was part of the military culture to drink socially, and I am certain my parents thought nothing of it. It was not until my niece expressed to me one day during a phone conversation years after Mom had passed that she believed her to be an alcoholic. I had never once entertained that thought prior to our conversation, but it dawned on me that perhaps she was right.

Things got particularly edgy between Mom and I in junior high. One day, Mom came home from work in a horrible mood. We had argued the night before about one of my friend's, Jilly. Jilly had run away from home, and her parents contacted mine asking if I knew where she had gone.

"You are going to tell me where Jilly is," Mom shouted at me, demanding an answer.

"No, I'm not!" I yelled back. "I don't know where she is. I told you that!" I said defiantly.

But I was lying. I knew where Jilly was. I was not about to tell on her. I ran down the hallway to my bedroom and heard Mom coming in behind me, fear clawing at my throat. She grabbed me by the shirt, yanking so hard that it ripped. Then she shoved me backwards onto my bed. I could smell cigarette smoke on her clothing and was terrified, yet angry and insolent. She began sobbing with frustration, leaning over me, jerking at my shirt. I just lay there, too afraid to move. My dad stayed out of it and was typically passive when such incidents occurred. I can only remember a couple times when he yelled at me and once slapped me across the face because I smarted off to him. I was stunned and started crying, and Dad immediately regretted what he had done, pulling me into an embrace. But, it was Mom I feared.

After I had my own daughter years later, I understood the kind of stress Mom endured and the pain she must have felt with no one to really support her emotionally. Looking back, I wondered if Mom struggled with undiagnosed depression, which might have explained her tirades and emotional highs and lows. There are others who have had far more difficult childhoods. I never hungered, I did not want for any physical needs. It was the tension in our home that was most difficult for me to cope with and caused me to fear others in authority. Dad did his best to be of help in our family, driving me to Girl Scout meetings and piano lessons, barbequing steaks on the weekends. But it must have been difficult for him, too, to tolerate the conflict in our home and in their marriage. Furthermore, my parents were not exactly equipped to help a child of a different race navigate through the intricacies of culture, race, and identity. I have often thought back on those days and wished that I could have been more of a support to Mom rather than a rebel. What would our family have been like if we had understood each other a little better? What if my parents had known how to initiate conversations about race and culture and were themselves, offered support? We never seemed to get on the same page.

At Mom's funeral, I did not think of those difficult times. I thought about how much she suffered because of the dementia. I wished that we could have been friends, as mothers and daughters often become, but my own pride and a terrible disease robbed us of that opportunity. Oddly, when I found my adoption contract, I felt Mom's presence. It was like a guiding presence. There was no fear, no anger. It took years to forgive my mother, but despite all the wrongs, I loved my parents and I know they loved me. I believed Mom and Dad would have wanted me to go and find the answers I sought. After all, they had kept my adoption contract and not thrown it away.

There is a scripture in the Bible that says the truth will set you free. At that moment, I was struck by an insatiable desire to search for my birth family. I longed to find the truth. I knew that only in finding the truth would I be set free.

寻找

Search

3.

Nothing happens unless first we dream.
~ Carl Sandburg

Nothing. My searches yielded absolutely nothing. It was maddening. No information whatsoever online about The Family Planning Association of China, the orphanage where I was adopted, or Tze-kuan Shu Kan, the Secretary General and Director. After finding my adoption contract and learning that I was Chinese, not Vietnamese or Japanese as my parents had told me, I was insanely curious about my origins. I became quickly discouraged as search after search failed. Darn Google! There were absolutely no leads on the world-wide web. This is how the search for my birth family began. Apparently, The Family Planning Association of China no longer existed. And why was I surprised? It had been over forty years since my adoption. I would be lucky to find any source of information readily, and yet I hoped. I was surprised and unprepared for the ways in which my search would take on a twisted life of its own.

On November 1, 2009, I would meet someone who would inspire me to keep searching and not give up. Someone who understood the complexities of international adoption, identity, race, and culture. Those individuals were truly rare. That morning, I attended a book signing at the Burton Barr Library in Phoenix held for a journalist and Taiwanese adoptee named Mei-Ling Hopgood. Mei-Ling was on tour to promote her new memoir, *Lucky Girl*. She was also adopted by a white American couple and reunited with her birth family in Taitung, Taiwan at the age of twenty-three. The Phoenix chapter of an organization called

Families with Children from China sponsored the event. Mei-Ling's book described her own fascinating search and reunion with her birth family. I was eager to hear Mei-Ling speak about her experience and had never met another adoptee from Taiwan. I knew plenty of adoptees from China, Korea, and India, but never Taiwan. Before the event, I jotted down a few questions I wanted to ask her in case I was too scatterbrained to remember.

The drive up to Phoenix was free of traffic. Although I lived in the area, I had never been to the Burton Barr library in Central Phoenix. The library touted the largest collection of books, DVD's, and CD's in the Phoenix Public Library system and featured an art collection displayed throughout its four levels. The library had an open and urban vibe, kind of like an old warehouse. Once arriving, I climbed the stairs to the room where the book signing was to be held. Rows of chairs were arranged with an aisle down the middle, and several families with their adopted children had already staked out seats near the front. White faces and little Asian ones scattered the room. Parents talked to one another in subdued voices, and it was apparent that they were part of a network of families who knew each other. I found a seat in an unoccupied section and sat down.

Soon, Mei-Ling walked down the aisle and took her seat in the front near a table where several of her books were stacked neatly, waiting to be signed. Mei-Ling was petite with a pretty face and smile. She was humble and friendly and discussed her book leisurely. I noticed that the adopted children, who ranged in age from very little to adolescent, clung to her every word, their eyes lit up like fireflies. I was the only other adult adoptee in the audience and certainly the only other one from Taiwan.

When her presentation was over, a long line of rapt children and adults formed, everyone waiting to either have their already purchased books signed, or to purchase a new one. Mei-ling patiently signed each book, engaging happily with her audience. I waited nervously in line towards the back. Although I had made a list of questions to ask Mei-Ling, I wanted to talk to her privately at greater length about her search. When it was my turn, I tried not to fumble over my words. I told Mei-Ling that I was searching for my birth family, but had made very little progress. She was exceedingly gracious and encouraged me to continue, signing my book, *"Lots of love & luck."* Several months later, I would write to Mei-Ling asking if Sister Maureen, the nun who acted as liaison between her birth and adoptive families and helped facilitate her adoption, might be able to assist me. Mei-Ling forwarded Sister Maureen's contact information without hesitation, although in the end, she was unable to provide much help, though she tried.

After meeting Mei-Ling, my mind was a whirl of impressions. I was more determined than ever to find my birth family. There had to be something or someone else out there who could help. Not long after the book signing, I was talking to my friend, Kathy, about Mei-Ling and her memoir, and she recommended that I contact Families with Children from China for suggestions. Kathy and her husband, Dave, had recently adopted a little girl from China. It was worth a try. I sent an email directly to the administrator of the organization. Shortly thereafter, the administrator, who was also an adoptive mom, provided me with the name of a social worker, Mei-Na Tien, who worked for an adoption agency in Washington State. Tien, as she later identified herself, got back to me quickly. I could not believe my lucky stars when she told me she was from Taiwan and spoke fluent Mandarin. I learned that she was the Program Director of Taiwan adoptions at a large adoption agency in Washington and worked specifically with families wanting to adopt children from Taiwan. My first contact with Tien occurred around December of 2009, just about a month after Mei-Ling's book signing event.

On December 23rd, I scanned my adoption contract and sent it to Tien realizing that chances were slim to none that either of my birth parents was still living. My birth mother was thirty-nine and birth father, fifty-five at the time of my birth, as I learned from my adoption contract. Still, I held out hope that my search, with Tien's assistance, would be fruitful. I waited expectantly for contact from Tien. When next I heard from her, she had read my adoption contract and provided partial answers to some of my most perplexing questions. Tien told me that my birth parents were originally from China. China, not Vietnam or Japan! For years I had explained to people that I was born in Taiwan, yet was really Japanese and Vietnamese and adopted by white parents. I further explained why I had a southern accent. It was a dialogue I had delivered countless times, much to my annoyance. A ripple of excitement flowed through every fiber of my body as I received confirmation of my true ethnicity. Indeed, I was Chinese! But, the question still lingered, why did my parents tell me I was Vietnamese and Japanese? Tien was just as baffled.

Tien agreed to take on my case free of any fees, despite my willingness to pay for her assistance. I was ecstatic. We began by investigating what happened to The Family Planning Association of China. Since she had ties in Taiwan, she recommended that I complete a power of attorney giving authorization to her helper in Taipei to obtain information about my birth family. Our initial correspondence began in January, 2010. On January 22nd, Tien wrote,

> *Our guy in Taiwan has checked the address for you. The address now has changed and the whole area has changed to commercial buildings. If (we) need to do more investigation then we need a POW from you to our helper so he can go to the registration dept. to dig (for) the information. If you would like to move forward, please let me know.*

Of course, I wanted to move forward, but what was a POW? Certainly not a prisoner of war. Tien's English was not always clear, so I asked her to clarify. She corrected herself and what she had meant to say was power of attorney. Ah, that made better sense. I asked to proceed with the power of attorney; however, I was concerned about the service fees. The fee for her helper in Taiwan was $200.00, and there was a smaller fee of $15.00 for the legalization process by the Taipei Economic and Cultural Office (TECO). Because our finances were tight, I was forced to delay sending the payment for a couple of months until I had saved enough. I promised Tien that I would send full payment then. On February 3rd, however, I received a message from Tien stating she was leaving on vacation to Taiwan and would take care of the power of attorney upon her return. I could wait to send the payment then.

"What?" I thought to myself sullenly. Leaving for vacation to Taiwan? We were just getting started! This was certainly an unwelcome interruption when we were just beginning to pick up some momentum. Nevertheless, I would just have to wait. In the meantime, I continued to dig for information on my own.

翻译

Translation

4.

Who in the world am I? Ah, that's the great puzzle.
~ Lewis Carroll, *Alice in Wonderland*

Tien gave no indication how long she would be away in Taiwan. I was disappointed that she left so suddenly, but reminded myself that she was helping me outside of work and on her own time. It was already March, and I hated to wait around for Tien's return. I was restless and had to do something. I thought of our neighbors next door, a Chinese family that we rarely spoke to. I walked across our driveway to our neighbor's house and sheepishly knocked on their door hoping someone would be kind enough to help translate my adoption contract. Although Tien had confirmed I was Chinese, I had many questions about my origins that I thought might be answered on my adoption contract, if only I could read it. There was surely a story there that Tien had not yet been able to share with me. As I stood there waiting for someone to answer the door, I studied a small red vase with intricately etched dragons and yellow flowers hanging next to the door. I had no idea if it had any significance or was there simply for decoration, but it was pretty. After several minutes, our neighbor, Mr. Hong, answered the door. My husband told me that Mr. Hong owned a Chinese food restaurant right down the street that the family helped run. I studied Mr. Hong's face. He looked to be in his mid to late fifties, his hair was sprinkled with silver. I tried to explain slowly why I had stopped by and was not sure how much Mr. Hong understood.

"Come back in half hour," he said in an accent, mildly interested. "My daughter-n-law be here then."

"Okay," I replied. "Thank you so much." I walked back home and busied myself around the house losing track of time until the doorbell rang an hour or so later. Our neighbor's youngest son, Alex, appeared in the doorway with his sister-in-law, Kelly. He introduced her to me and explained that she did not speak English, but together they would be happy to assist in interpreting my papers - later. Later? Alex had class that afternoon. I reluctantly gave him a Xeroxed copy of my adoption contract, regretful he had to hurry off. Alex and Kelly did not return that evening.

The following night, however, our doorbell rang again. It was Alex and Kelly. Kelly was very thin, her long hair pulled back in a ponytail, and appeared to be in her early twenties. Alex was a handsome young man, probably nineteen or twenty and was dressed in jeans and a hoodie. He was completing his business degree at Arizona State University. Both were friendly and helpful. After showing them in, we gathered around the dinner table with the copy of my adoption contract, and the translation began. Kelly looked at the contract and began speaking rapidly, using her finger to mark where she read. I sat on the edge of my chair wishing I could understand what she was saying. Every so often Alex interjected in Mandarin to ask a question and nodded his head as Kelly explained. Finally, Alex turned to me. He pointed to one section of the contract.

"This section explains the history of why your birth parents gave you up for adoption," he said. "Your parents were very poor and there was no money in the household. You were the fourth daughter from a large family, and they had to relinquish one girl to adoption, the youngest, which was you." I wondered if I were born a boy, would my parents have kept me and if they had been disappointed that another girl was born into the family. Did they waiver over the decision to relinquish me? So many questions raced through my mind. Was I placed in the orphanage immediately following my birth, or did I stay with my family for some period of time? The answers to these questions were not disclosed on the pages of my adoption contract.

Alex continued and next brought my attention to a different area of the contract. He pointed to some Mandarin characters and circled them.

"These are your birth parent's names," he said matter-of-factly. I examined the characters more closely as though such deliberate scrutiny would somehow connect me to my birth parents wherever they were. All the characters looked so similar. How would I ever learn to recognize their Chinese names, my own Chinese name?

"Your parents are from a province in China called Guangxi," Alex continued. "It's in south China, like Hong Kong." He wrote out the name of the city phonetically, "Gong-sai," so that I would remember how to pronounce it. Later, I learned that Guangxi had a population of around 45 million people and was made up of several ethnic groups. The region bordered Vietnam.

"Hmm," I thought out loud. "Maybe there's some connection here between what my parents told me about being half Vietnamese."

"Maybe," Alex said. "That's very interesting."

"I wonder how my birth family ended up in Taiwan?" I mused.

"Maybe the orphanages were better in Taiwan and your birth parents placed you there to increase your chances of being adopted," Alex replied.

"Huh. I would never have thought of that," I answered. That was as good a guess as any.

After the translation, Alex and Kelly assured me that my adoption was legally agreed upon by both my birth and adoptive parents.

"You know," Alex said, "traditional Chinese families typically stay in one house their whole lives, so chances are, your family still lives in Taiwan at the same address. Their address would be fairly easy to locate if you were ever to travel there."

"Really? Well that's good to know," I replied, hopeful.

I thanked Alex and Kelly for their kind help as the evening came to a close. They wished me good luck in my search, happy to have been of help.

After they left, I poured over everything Alex and Kelly told me. It was frustrating not having all the pieces, and I did not have a clear understanding of how I arrived in Taiwan. And yet, I was blown away by the fact that I was Chinese. It was true. I was most certainly not Japanese and Vietnamese. All this time, my parents had been mistaken. What happened? I was paralyzed with disbelief, yet fascinated by my "new" identity. I began googling Taiwanese women on the Internet to compare my facial features to theirs. Did I have the same shape eyes? The same skin tone? What about my nose? My search led me to Taiwanese actresses and models. Ziyi Zhang, Ariel Lin, Barbie Hsu, Vivian Hsu, Shu Qi. The list went on. They were all so young and beautiful. And thin. God-awful thin. *"I should not compare myself to these women,"* I told myself. Clearly, they were not representative of all Taiwanese females. I showed the images I had found to my husband.

"Do you think I look like any of these women?" I asked Pat.

"Well, maybe," he said half interested. He was amused at my sudden absorption with Taiwanese women. I knew it was weird, but could not help myself, and we joked about it. Lexie, our daughter who was then thirteen years old, asked, "So, *what* am I?"

"Well, you're part Vietnamese, Japanese, and Chinese," I explained. "Dad is Japanese and Vietnamese, and I'm Chinese now. Well, actually I've always been Chinese, but just learned about it." I laughed at the absurdity of it.

"Oh, okay," she replied, puzzled. "I just want to make sure I get it straight when someone asks me." I could certainly understand and appreciate her confusion.

"Who in the world am I?" I thought. I felt like Alice in Wonderland after she had drunk the Drink Me potion and morphed into a giant. What I had always believed and come to know about myself shattered. What would I unravel next? Could I piece together my identity and figure out what had led my adoptive parents to be so mistaken? I knew that I needed Tien's help. So, I clung to the hope of her return. There was nothing else I could do but wait.

日记

Diary

5.

To respect a mystery is to make way for the answer.
~ Criss Jami

The weeks dragged by with no word from Tien. I occupied myself with investigating as much as I could outside of work, searching for any hint of a clue here and there. On March 23rd, I received a large package from Margaret back in Louisiana. I had asked her to find Mom's diaries and send them to me in hopes they might provide some missing pieces related to my adoption. I lugged the cardboard box in, grabbed a pair of scissors and began cutting away at the tape. Styrofoam peanuts flew out as I dug to the bottom of the box. Margaret found three diaries, although I knew more existed. One diary was dated 1943-1946, another 1962-1966. I immediately grabbed the latter one and started reading, my heart racing. I devoured each page until I found what I was looking for. Apparently my parents began entertaining thoughts of adoption around January of 1966. Mom's diary entry on January 21st read,

> *"Janie and I went to Machoriato to the Souls Episcopalian Church and Father Stough to talk about the baby. Not too much help but certainly believe he'll help..."*

I had no idea what "Machoriato" was, but Googled the church Mom referred to and found an All Souls Anglican Church and Mission in Taipei. From what I could tell, it fit the description of the church Mom talked about in her diary. I sent an email hoping to find out and no more than half an hour later, received an email from Fr. Larry Kirchner stating that indeed it was the same church, and there was a Fr. Stough during that time. The next entry referring to "the baby" was dated February 1, 1966,

> *Janie came up very early – Father Stough called that he had a little 3 yr. old boy, then it turned out to be a girl for me to see. Janie almost hit a kid on Kadena AFB."*

I chuckled as I read about Janie's poor driving skills. Janie was my godmother and Mom's confidante at Kadena Air Force base in Okinawa. She was a petite, Japanese woman with short dark hair, but had a giant personality and endearing accent. My parents met her and her husband, Nelson, on the base, and they were beloved family friends. Janie and Nelson eventually moved to Delaware, and on occasion, visited us in Louisiana years later. When we still lived on the military base at Barksdale, Kevin, their teenaged son, babysat me while our parents went out. Kevin was dreadful and must have resented having to look after me. He insisted on playing hide-and-go-seek and hid in our big two-storied military house, jumping out from behind the draperies or some other obscure place to scare me as I searched for him. It was as though he took great pleasure in seeing my frightened face.

Janie once visited our home in Sun City. I was probably around the age of eight or nine. She painted my fingernails and made me a velvety brown jumper on Mom's sewing machine. I fell in love with her and sobbed the day she left. I had an especially difficult time when anyone I felt close to said good-bye. When my Dad left for business trips a couple days at a time, the anxiety I felt caused physical illness. At the airport, I would not get out of the car with Mom to walk Janie in because I was too embarrassed by all of my sobbing. Long after I moved from Louisiana to Florida, Janie and Nelson visited me where I lived in Orlando. I was in my early twenties, and we went to lunch together. Janie was as spunky as ever. She and Nelson paid for my lunch, which was a real treat. I was always broke in those days, barely scraping by as a studio tour guide at Universal Studios Orlando. I never saw Janie or Nelson after that day and often wondered what became of them. I attempted to find them via

Facebook and through Google searches, although none of my searches yielded any information.

Father Stough contacted Mom again on February 3, 1966, to tell her about "a baby," for adoption, and they set a date the following Monday to meet the little girl. After seeing her, Mom wrote on February 7, 1966,

> *We go to see the little girl. Went to Naha to see her – she was beautiful – absolutely as pretty a child as I ever saw in my life. We were so disappointed that the Grandma didn't want to give her up. Janie and Nelson brought me home.*

I can only imagine the disappointment Mom felt. I wondered where Dad was as Mom and Janie were off visiting orphanages, most likely at work. The next entry related to adopting a baby did not occur until two months later on April 28, 1966. Mom heard about an Okinawan girl expecting a baby; however, nothing came of it. Then on May 21, 1966, Mom talked about adopting a child from Taiwan. Until that point, she had only searched for adoptable children in Okinawa. Mom wrote on May 21, 1966,

> *Rains so heavy. Heard about getting a baby in Taiwan...*

In June, the following month, she wrote a letter about "getting a baby from Taiwan" followed soon after by another letter to the U.S. government with a power of attorney enabling her and Dad to become legal guardians of a minor. I found the receipt for payment dated December 20, 1966, from the Department of State, United States of America in the box with my adoption contract. My parents would wait another month for more news about adopting a child from Taiwan. Finally, on August 8, 1966, word came back:

> *...Got letter from Mr. Forbes in Taipei, Taiwan...*

It was unclear to me as I read Mom's diary if the long wait to adopt from Taiwan was due to the process of adoption itself or Mom was uncertain what to do, and I did not know who Mr. Forbes was.

Mom did not mention him again, but I assumed he worked for the adoption agency. Today, it can take up to two or three years to adopt a child overseas depending on the country. On November 25, 1966, three months after Mom first spoke of adopting from Taiwan, she wrote,

> *...Maybe we'll go to Taiwan soon...*

Three weeks later, Mom and Dad left for Taiwan. She wrote on December 15, 1966,

> *Left Kadena AFB for Taipei, Taiwan. Went to Family Planning. Saw Chaling. Had interview with Mrs. Kan. Chaling was brought to us. Such a beautiful baby. Faulkenburgs with us. Went out to see and meet Miss Radley and Susie.*

I was Chaling; it was the middle name given to me by my adoptive parents, and The Faulkenburgs were a military couple at Kadena who also adopted a child in Taipei from another orphanage. I wondered who Miss Radley and Susie were. Mom mentioned Susie in one of her later diary entries, but never Miss Radley. After I found my adoption contract, I found an old letter from a nun addressed to my parents about Carmen, the Faulkenburg's adopted daughter, who was around the age of four when she was adopted. The orphanage where Carmen was adopted was operated by nuns. I learned that my parents were Carmen's godparents. When we lived in Louisiana, the Faulkenburg's came to visit us at our home on LaNell Street in Bossier City. We lived in this house before moving to the home on Pluto Drive where I grew up most of my childhood. Carmen was a very pretty little girl, and I remember wanting to look more like her because of her slender nose and beautiful hair.

On Friday, December 16, 1966, my parents completed the paperwork to adopt me from The Family Planning Association of China. Mom wrote,

> *Started the paperwork for Marijane Chaling Buck – raining. Finished at the Court House by 5 pm. Then*

we all went out to eat. Took the baby to 7th D. Adventist Hospital. She checked out OK.

I found wrinkled receipts my parents kept from a hospital in Taipei called the Taiwan Sanitarium and Hospital. My adoption, in addition to the physical examination, cost my parents $559.00 including vaccinations, medications, the consultation and doctor's visit. I wondered if the Seventh Day Adventist Hospital Mom mentioned in her diary and the Taiwan Sanitarium where I was given the exam were somehow connected? I went to the Internet and found that they were indeed one and the same hospital. The Taiwan Adventist Hospital was one of over 600 healthcare institutions operated by the Seventh-Day Adventist Church in a worldwide mission. The Hospital was originally relocated from Shanghai to Taipei in 1949. It was then re-established as the Taiwan Sanitarium Hospital by its founder only to be renamed the Taiwan Sanitarium and Hospital some years later after the hospital experienced significant growth. In 1971, the hospital underwent further development and became the Taiwan Adventist Hospital. There was no connection to my parent's faith and the Seventh Day Adventist church. My mom was Catholic and dad, Pentecostal. When I was a little girl, however, we attended a Methodist church for some years. After my parents stopped going to church, they sent my niece and I to a Baptist church, and we caught a little red church bus every Sunday for Sunday school.

The days following my official adoption on December 16, 1966, only four months after my birth, were quite busy according to Mom. They stayed in Taipei a few more days trying to finalize everything before returning to Okinawa and the military base. Mom wrote,

Run – run – trying to get things done. Everything closes at noon in Taiwan. Took train to Yan Shui to St. Benedicts'. Beautiful. Enjoyed meeting the sisters.

Spent a little time shopping. Then stayed out at the Hosp. Visited with Susie. She's a darling.

St. Benedicts was the orphanage where Carmen Faulkenburg was adopted. I assumed that Susie, whom Mom mentioned previously, was one of the nuns at the orphanage. The orphanage at St. Benedict's no longer exists today and is currently a monastery where special events and conventions are held for nuns.

After reading Mom's diary entries, I had so many questions. In one of her last entries, Mom stated that all the adoption paperwork had been completed. She and Dad left Taiwan for Okinawa on December 19th, three days after my adoption. Mom wrote,

> *Wendy and Alice Lee run all day – got our papers finished. Baby vaccinated. Spent all day running with Esther and Susie to find baby clothes. Not too much luck. The Faulkenburgs left. Shopped a bit. Met Col. Richmond – helped us get on S/A plane. Arrived at Kadena at 2 AM. Baby very good. Mickey and Barney here – Lee and Dan got up to see baby. Girls very pleased.*

My parents never talked about Alice Lee or Col. Richmond, Mickey, Barney, Lee or Dan. I assume they were friends of the family at Kadena Air Force base. The "girls" my mom referred to were my two half sisters, Margaret, who took care of Mom while she had Alzheimer's disease, and Jessica. Jessica was Dad's only daughter from his previous marriage.

After getting the "new baby settled in," the 4252nd wing gave Mom a baby shower at the military base. Mom wrote, *"I got everything for Marijane. It was so nice."* She saved all the baby shower cards from that day. The tiny cards lay buried with my adoption contract, pretty pink, purple, yellow, and blue pastels faded with age. Mom wrote,

> *Our baby girl is with us. So precious. Went to the "Little Club" for Xmas Dinner. Marijane very good. Girls had a good Xmas. A very happy day for all.*

The "little club" was the Officer's Club on the military base. After reading Mom's diary, I could not help but wonder how I adjusted to my new family. I am sure that English was foreign to my ears. I was only four months old. Did I attach quickly to my adoptive parents? Did I fuss? What did my new sisters think of me, and where were my half-brothers? I had three of them. More so, did my birth parents and biological family mourn the loss of their youngest member? That is what kept me awake at night the most, wondering.

Mom's diary was one more piece of the puzzle. I sat on the floor of our dining room with her diary in my hands, a small ache throbbing in my chest. I attempted to fill in the gaps with my own imagination. None of this would have been as stunning had my parents shared what they knew with me - my adoption contract, my history, and our early lives together at Kadena AFB. After all, thousands of babies have been adopted from overseas, many never learning anything about their origins. What made my situation unique was being told one thing about my past by my parents and then learning years later it was erroneous. I knew deep inside that some of the missing pieces were in Taiwan, with my birth family, if they were still alive. There had to be a way to get to them.

信件

Letter

6.

*Imagine waking up one morning and finding a piece
of yourself you didn't even know existed.*
~ Jodi Picoult, *Nineteen Minutes*

Mom's diary helped fill in some of the gaps. I was to find yet another important artifact, however, that gave me an even deeper glimpse into my past. It was contained inside a plain old manila folder. The folder had settled beneath dozens of scattered pictures and styrofoam peanuts in the same box Margaret had sent. Inside the folder was a letter, quite fragile and yellowed with age. I recognized the embellished handwriting immediately as that of my mom's. Curiosity set in as I wondered who the mysterious recipient was.

The letter was not dated and was obviously a draft, as many of the words had been crossed out. Apparently, Mom had written the letter as a follow up to a conversation previously held with a physician named Dr. Woo. After reading through the first paragraph, I soon realized that this letter described my parents' initial visit to the Family Planning Association of China, the orphanage where I was adopted. I could not read the letter fast enough. This is what it said,

> Dr. Woo –
> Following our ~~conversation~~ adopted Chinese
> daughter's visa physical, and our conversation as ~~to
> what was~~ where we obtained her, and the ~~cash~~ price
> we paid, I will attempt to explain the procedure and all

the obstacles that confront an American who adopts a child from the Family Planning Association of China.

We arrived in Taipei at 10 AM – went directly to Family Planning. We were allowed to go immediately to the 4th floor to a huge room with open windows and no heat where we walked from crate to crate and from basket to basket looking at tiny babies. I chose two from the 26 that were adoptable that day.

At 4 o' clock that evening we were ushered into a large office and were introduced to Mrs. Tze-kuan Shu Kan. She stated she had just returned from a fundraising drive in the United States and had acquired $30,000 to start building a new orphanage for her children. She stated that $250 was the minimum fee, which was $150 for prior care of the child (medical, food and lodging) and $100 was for the cost of all the paper work required to bring the po baby to Okinawa. This was to be pd. in American cash.

By 6 o' clock – the necessary papers were signed and she asked if I had picked out a baby. I told her about the two I had chosen and which one they brought down was all right with us. In a few moments they brought our baby to us, a beautiful three month old, 7 lbs., 7 oz., and very listless baby girl. I could not stand to think she would stay another moment under their roof. I asked permission...

The letter abruptly ended. I knew that the listless baby girl Mom referred to was me; however, there appeared to be a missing page or two. I went back to the box and searched intently for the remainder of the letter, but to my great dismay, found nothing. Where was the rest of the letter? I was intrigued and seriously disappointed that there was nothing further, just a draft of a letter. Did Mom ever complete the letter? Did she eventually send it to Dr. Woo? Most curious of all, Mom referred to me as "our adopted Chinese daughter." She knew! She knew I was Chinese. Why did my parents tell me that I was Vietnamese and Japanese? It did not make any sense at all. I telephoned Margaret back in Louisiana to ask if she knew about the letter and knew where the missing parts were. She knew nothing. I had to just accept the fact that the other half of the letter was gone. It seemed as though I was met with disappointment at every corner. Missing pages to letters and scant diary entries left me frustrated and wanting more.

Questions lit up my mind like shooting stars. Did I go home with my parents that evening? What did Mom ask permission for? What were the "obstacles" she referred to when adopting from the Family Planning Association of China? Who was Dr. Woo? From Mom's description of the orphanage, I envisioned it to be in poor condition most likely due to a lack of funding. She mentioned that there were twenty-six babies available to adopt the day she and Dad visited the orphanage. Were there more children who lived at the orphanage who were not available to adopt? That I was only seven pounds and seven ounces at the age of three months was proof that the babies were malnourished and resources were scare. Again, I questioned my parent's story about my adoption. It was more confusing than ever. I was left to wonder why; why did they tell me I was Vietnamese and Japanese? This continued to haunt me day after day.

I went back to read Mom's diary. She did not mention Dr. Woo, but only how they brought me home from Taiwan to Okinawa, and even that narrative was meager. I searched the contents of the manila folder again finding a medical examination form signed by Dr. Woo. It was dated June 28, 1968, nearly two years after my adoption. It dawned on me that my parents needed to obtain a visa so I could travel back to the U.S. one day, and perhaps it was Dr. Woo who gave the exam required. My father was reassigned to the U.S. about two years after my adoption. We eventually moved to Massachusetts from Okinawa and lived at Westover Air Force base for a spell. I do not know how long we lived at Westover except that I attended preschool there. We then moved to Louisiana where I grew up for most of my childhood.

I was curious about the incomplete letter to Dr. Woo and disappointed that the rest was lost. It shed some light, however dim, on the orphanage where I was adopted, on the very early days of my life. I was stunned that my parents apparently knew that I was Chinese. I was finding little pieces of myself that I did not know even existed.

Later that week, I was outside sweeping our driveway, and our neighbor, Mr. Hong, and Alex, his son, were outside. Alex and Kelly had helped to interpret my adoption contract just a week previous. We exchanged hellos and Alex's father asked if I was Chinese. In the past, I would have told him without hesitation that I was Vietnamese and Japanese. It felt good to tell him that I was indeed Chinese, from Taiwan. I explained to him that I was adopted and searching for my birth family in China. He told me that he would be traveling to China soon and that his brother worked for the government there. He offered to help find my birth family and could use the address listed on my adoption contract as a starting point. He thought his brother could assist because of his position in the government. Mr. Hong would be staying in Guangzhou, a province very close to Guangxi, the province of my birthparents. I was touched that he wanted to help and gladly accepted his offer. There was nothing else to do now except continue waiting for Tien's return and hope that our neighbor came home with some good news.

挫折

Wall

7.

Every wall is a door.
~ Ralph Waldo Emerson

Nothing eventful occurred after I read my mom's diary and the mysterious letter to Dr. Woo. The weeks dragged on. I waited none too patiently for some word from Tien and hoped she had not forgotten me. When the heck was she coming back? Then on May 10, 2010, three months after my last correspondence with her, I received an email. Tien had finally returned to the States. She wrote:

> *I am so sorry that I have not responded back to you after I backed from Taiwan. Just let me know if you still need me to help you on this matter after your friend backed from China.*

A rush of relief poured over me. The "friend" Tien referred to was Mr. Hong, our next door neighbor. I wrote back to Tien immediately. By the time Tien had returned, Mr. Hong had also returned from his trip to China. I was disappointed that he had not contacted me to share any news about my birth family, good or bad. Tien informed me that it would not have been easy for him to find any information because my adoption took place so many years ago, and furthermore, a civil war had occurred in Mainland China, but she did not elaborate. I was not sure how the civil war played into any search attempts for my birth family, so I conducted some research and Googled "civil war in China." I learned that the civil war Tien referred to was the Chinese Civil

War that lasted from 1927 to 1950. There was a long-standing history of political conflict in China between the Kuomintang, or Chinese Nationalist Party, and the Communist Party of China. The two parties fought primarily over idealistic differences. Hostilities officially ended many years later following the end of World War Two. By then, the Communist Party of China had gained control of Mainland China and this led to the establishment of the Peoples Republic of China. Those loyal to the Kuomintang, were forced to leave China and fled to the island of Taiwan where they formed a new government, The Republic of China (ROC), recognized today as Taiwan. Current relations between China and Taiwan remain delicate primarily due to conflict over Taiwan's independence from China and China's claim that there is only one China, which includes the territory of Taiwan. I thought perhaps the war affected my birth family in some way, but was not sure. Maybe one day I would find out.

Over the next couple of weeks, Tien and I sent numerous emails back and forth as she instructed me on how to complete the consent for power of attorney. It was a tedious process. Tien had to translate the information I sent to her to Mandarin. Inevitably, corrections had to be made, or Tien would notify me that she needed further information. She was required to send the power of attorney to the Taiwan Economic and Cultural Office (TECO) prior to notarization. It was all very confusing, but I trusted Tien and let her work her magic. TECO also needed my original baby passport issued in Taiwan after my adoption. The name on my passport was Baby Marijane Chaling Buck. I was afraid to send the actual passport, but was reassured that I would eventually receive it back. This we hoped would provide enough proof of relation to my birth family. At the end of May 2010, and after Tien's careful review, I sent the package with power of attorney and my baby passport to TECO in Taipei hoping that these items would give Tien's helper access to the information we needed.

Nearly a month passed without any news regarding the consent for power of attorney. I waited with anticipation and told myself that these things took time. There were huge differences in time zones, and anything related to government proceedings, whether here or overseas, always moved at an exasperatingly slow pace. No news was good news, right? I needed to be patient. On June 20, 2010, I decided to contact Tien just to touch bases. What she told me was not exactly what I wanted to hear. Her team checked with the registration office and was told that the power of attorney was insufficient to procure what we sought. TECO would not provide an address or any further information. The clerk said that TECO would attempt to contact my birth parents or relatives first and ask if they wanted to contact me directly. Tien told me that her helper would check with other registration offices to see if there might be a different way to obtain information. After reading Tien's email, my next thought was to contact TECO myself. But Tien informed me that it would be impossible to speak directly to one of the numerous clerks there due to the language barrier.

I read Tien's entire email letting the words sink in. "*...Even if they have the POA they still won't provide the address or other information to our Taiwan person. Initially, I thought it should not be too difficult to get the information as long as we had the POA, but now it seems not that easy. It might take time to find the right way to get the information.*" My heart sank a little at the implications. We had come up against a wall. Before, we had been so sure the power of attorney would open doors. I had imagined Tien eagerly telling me that her "Taiwan person" had found my birth family. I envisioned my excitement in response to the happy news. Sadly, this was not the case. That would have been too easy. By the end of June 2010, we were no closer to finding my birth family than when we had first set out five months previous. We did not know if they still lived in Taipei. Was our trail cold? How could TECO withhold such information? I had proof that my birth family existed in Taipei and that I belonged to them at one time. We were at the mercy of some clerk in Taipei who might or might not make attempts to contact my birth family. My hopes quickly deflated. Despite the abrupt setback, I held onto the fact that it was still very early in the search. I would not let this temporary setback dissuade me. I would trust Tien to formulate a new plan.

* * *

After the unsuccessful attempt to obtain information about my birth family from the Taiwan Economic and Cultural Office, the frequency in communication between Tien and I rapidly decreased. I knew she was busy with work at the adoption agency, and yet I was still eager to continue our search. The momentum had certainly diminished. I would not hear again from Tien for a period of roughly four months.

In early October 2010, Tien contacted me. She recommended a new course of action and suggested that I write an announcement, like a newspaper ad, stating that I was searching for my birth family. She would help with the translation and submit the announcement to a local newspaper in Taipei. It seemed like a reasonable plan, although the better solution by far would be to travel to Taiwan and search for records in person. Tien had even invited me to accompany her on her next trip to Taipei early the following January. Her father still lived there, and she visited each Lunar or Chinese New Year. As much as I wanted to travel with her, I knew it was an impossibility. We did not have the finances to support such a trip, and I dared not let myself entertain the thought knowing that it would only lead to more disappointment. I had also just started a new job as a music therapist, and it would have been difficult to get time off work. My new job soon became a welcome distraction from all the ambiguity surrounding the search for my birth family.

I waited for Tien to send some direction concerning the newspaper announcement. What should I say? Woman in search of birth family who was adopted by Americans forty plus years ago? We were not even certain anyone from my birth family still lived in Taipei, and for that matter, was still living at all. I had reservations about Tien's new plan, but what were the alternatives? We were working against time differences, government bureaucracy, and a passage of time that had occurred so many years earlier. Would advertising in the local Taipei newspaper spark any interest locally? Would we be successful in reaching my birth family or someone, anyone acquainted with them? The likelihood seemed one in a million. I felt overwhelmed with the enormity of finding my family in a population of millions of people. What were the odds? As questionable as Tien's plan seemed, it was my only hope.

* * *

Week after week flew by without any response from Tien. The last email I received from her was dated June 28, 2010. Again, I reminded myself that she was busy. She would get back to me when she could. However, weeks turned to months, and the months wore on without so much as a whisper from Tien. What happened? We were going to place an announcement in a local Taipei newspaper about my search in the hopes of reaching a member of my birth family. I had no idea how to proceed. Did Tien decide that the obstacles were too great? Was she just busier than usual?

The holidays soon approached. Halloween, Thanksgiving, Christmas. Still no word. By the end of the year, I assumed that the engine had run out of steam. The search was over. I was confounded by the silence, but I was not ready to give up. As a new year approached, however, the hope of ever finding my birth family dwindled. I lamented, hiding my disappointment from others. My priorities changed, and I poured all my energies into work and family. *"What did you expect?"* I asked myself. *Did you really think you could find your birth family after all these years?"* With every passing month, I grew increasingly apathetic until the search became nothing more than an obscure memory. Yet every so often, I wondered if it were still possible to find them. I dared not allow myself to hope.

曙光

Light

8.

From the ashes a fire shall be woken, a light
from the shadows shall spring...
~ J.R.R. Tolkien, *The Fellowship of the Ring*

The New Year rung in woefully, and a new season advanced. Easter was right around the corner when, to my great surprise, I received an unexpected yet welcome message from an unknown sender via my blog, *Beyond Two Worlds*. On April 22, 2011, a Taiwanese adoptee named Ma-Li wrote:

> *Do the words Family Planning Association of China, Taipei City mean anything to you? I was adopted at the age of three via that organisation, but unlike you got delivered to London, Heathrow in the summer of 1970. The thought of going back to recover the lost, forgotten roots of my beginnings has been with me for a very long time.*

Family Planning of Association of China caught my immediate attention. I held my breath. Could it be that this writer was adopted from the same orphanage? For the first time in a long while, I permitted myself to be curious again. It appeared that another adoptee had reached out from halfway across the universe. I clicked on the link leading to Ma-Li's blog, *PoetJena,* and emailed her at once. We continued to exchange emails and scheduled a time to talk via Skype. Ma-Li lived in Germany between the cities of Weimer and Erfurt. I was intrigued by her story and wanted to know more. On Easter morning, April 24, 2011, Ma-Li attempted to call me, but due to the time difference, I missed her call. Naturally, I was disappointed, but she left a voicemail message, and I admired her charming British accent. When we finally connected, Ma-Li showed me an old business card that she had kept through the years. She held it up to the computer screen so that I could see the name Tze-kuan Shu Kan clearly. Ms. Kan was the director of The Family Planning Association of China. I had recovered a similar business card with the same name and title among my adoption papers. What a remarkable coincidence. We were both adopted from the very same orphanage! Suddenly, I did not feel so alone anymore in my pursuit to connect to my cultural roots.

Ma-Li and I talked as long as we could before I had to leave for work. We compared histories, which were strikingly similar. Ma-Li was adopted by an older British couple in 1970, four years after my adoption, and was raised in the United Kingdom. I was adopted by an older American couple, but raised in the United States. Ma-Li's adoptive father was a pilot in the Second World War and served in the Royal Air Force. Interestingly, he flew a Supermarine Spitfire. My father was also a pilot, but in the US Army Air Corp and flew a B-24 Liberator. I wondered if our fathers ever crossed paths somewhere up in the big blue. Ma-Li explained that her parents were terribly old-fashioned and strict as were mine. Her parents were also deceased. We talked about the difficulties of growing up looking different from everyone else around us. She, too, struggled with issues related to identity, an Asian face that stood out among the crowd of white. We were close to the same age, although Ma-Li was a year younger than me. She learned from her adoption contract that her birth father abandoned her family and she was, therefore, relinquished because of her birth mother's inability to properly care for her. Ma-Li also felt strongly that she had biological siblings somewhere unknown to her. I was regretful that we did not have more time to chat.

Ma-Li was the first Taiwanese adoptee from the same orphanage that I had ever made contact with. It was monumental to encounter another adoptee who shared such similar roots. We continue to keep in touch to this day, and Ma-Li eventually moved to the States. Ma-Li was like a beacon shining brightly through the gloomy clouds of disappointment. She gave me the courage I needed to continue my search. I could not give up no matter how long it took. She understood that desire to connect to our cultural roots, to make sense of our adoption journeys and the impact of it on our lives. Talking to Ma-Li was like talking to an old friend, a kindred spirit. Her reaching out broke through the long silence that had penned me in. I felt a renewed sense of hope that would carry me through the next stretch.

希望

Hope

9.

*Hope is the thing with feathers that perches in the soul - and
sings the tunes without the words - and never stops at all.*
~ Emily Dickinson

I wrote to Tien occasionally during that long period of silence.
When my emails went unanswered, however, I stopped. What use was
it? As time marched on, life became routine and predictable, and I fell
right into step. Work. Family. Eat. Sleep. And do it all again the next
day. After a year of no communication with Tien, the search for my
birth family came to a screeching halt and was all but forgotten. One
summer morning late in July 2011, however, I woke to find a message
from Tien waiting for me. What a welcome surprise! What news could
she possibly bear? First, she stated that she had not forgotten me. Thank
God. She then gave me the news that I had been waiting so long to hear.
Tien told me that she had found one of my biological sisters through the
registration office in Taipei while on visit to Taiwan. I gasped. Could
it be true? I wanted to believe that the woman Tien thought to be my
biological sister was truly a blood relative, yet was unconvinced, mostly
afraid that it was too good to be true. The registration office would not
release any further information about my sister because Tien was not
biologically related. Really, it was quite remarkable that Tien had been
able to finagle any particulars at all from the registration office about
my birth family. This was indeed progress by leaps and bounds.

Tien then told me that both of my birth parents had passed away
some time ago. My previous assumptions had been correct. I wondered
how long ago they had died? I would later grieve this loss, but at that

moment, was too caught up in the news that I had a living relative in Taipei. Because the registration office refused to offer any other information, Tien advised me to contact a special agency in Taipei, The Child and Juvenile Information Center which provided reunion services specifically to Taiwanese adoptees. She assured me that this agency would continue to assist me in finding my birth family.

I followed the link Tien provided to The Child and Juvenile Information Center, and on July 28, 2011, sent an email informing the agency of my search. I gave them my birthparent's names and said that I had been adopted from the Family Planning Association of China in Taipei. I told them about Tien and how she had found my biological sister in Taipei. I also requested that Tien be permitted to continue assisting with the search. I was grateful to receive an email from the agency later that same evening and was told to complete the application for reunion service on their website and mail the required documents, including my adoption contract. Once received, they would begin the searching work. I was ready to make a copy of my adoption contract, but I could not find it. We had moved earlier in the year, and the box that I had placed the document in was missing! I searched everywhere, the garage, all the closets, my husband's office, to no avail. I was frantic and quickly emailed Tien to ask if she had kept a copy of the contract. Thankfully, she had a copy and sent it to me. On August 3, 2011, I sent the application for reunion service and copy of my adoption contract to the Child and Juvenile Information Center. The next morning, the agency notified me that they were missing the "household document," apparently a part of the adoption contract and the most vital record needed to complete the search. I was not sure what the agency was referring to, but set out at once determined to find my original adoption contract and the household document. My husband was eventually able to locate the right box, and I found a document, written completely in Mandarin, that had been inserted into my adoption contract. I was sure this was the document the agency needed. I scanned it and sent it straight to the agency. Disappointingly, this document was not the one they required. As a result, the agency requested a copy of my current passport or driver's license to prove my identity. Once the agency received copies, they could start the reunion process. Another snag. I made a copy of my driver's license and forwarded it. I was afraid that this agency would similarly deny me any information because of all the bureaucracy related to proving who I was. It was all very complicated due to distance, language, and the obligatory procedures, and I did not want to lose momentum. I longed to travel to Taiwan to finish the search in person. It would be far easier, I thought.

A week later, an agency worker named Agnes notified me that the searching process *"could take a while"* because I was unable to provide an "ID number" and the household document. What ID number was she referring to? Was it some kind of identification number given to the babies at the orphanage? Agnes ended her message by asking for my patience and said she would contact me as soon as she had any news.

A couple of weeks later, Agnes sent the following email:

> *We received some information from the household system; it's about your birth parents. As your blog mentioned, your birth parents passed away, your birth father was died in 2008, and your birth mother was died in 1998, we are deeply sorry about this information. About the member in your birth family, we now have some information but still need time to check if we do find the right person, please be patient for our following contact.*

Agnes only confirmed what I already knew about my birthparents. Yet, the reality of never meeting them sank in fully. It suddenly hit me with a force that I had not expected. I mourned for days, deeply saddened by this loss. I wondered what my birthparents had looked like? Did I resemble them in any way? Why did they relinquish me? I thought about my birth mother and what she might have felt following my absence. I was shocked by my own grief. How could I mourn for those I had never met? And then I understood. A part of me had also died. It seemed almost ludicrous that I would never meet the two individuals who gave life to me. I was overanalyzing things, yet in that moment, adoption seemed to bring nothing but loss. I felt the impact of that loss in a way I had never experienced before. I had always been so accepting of my adoption. It was a fact; it was my life. But now I felt such loss that it took my breath away. I sat on the edge of our bathtub and cried. I let myself grieve for some time. I embraced it, and through the grief, I imagined my birthparents urging me forward. I imagined them saying, *"Don't give up. You're almost there. Just take one tiny step at a time."* And that is what I resolved to do.

It became a matter of urgency to find my biological sister. We were so close, yet the barriers continued to surmount at every turn. I was once again at the mercy of others to contact my birth family. Despite the challenges, I held out hope that one day in the near future, I would meet my family, and with each passing day, that hope grew a little stronger.

时间与耐心

Time & Patience

10.

The strongest of all warriors are these two — Time and Patience.
~ Leo Tolstoy, *War and Peace*

I continued to keep Tien updated on the progress made by the Child and Juvenile Information Center in Taipei. Our emails flew back and forth almost weekly like a flurry of snow on a blustery winter day. Agnes, the agency worker who took on my case in Taiwan, was friendly and responsive, yet I could not help but feel as though time were standing still. Progress seemed slow and her emails came less frequently. The hardest part was waiting. I had waited this long, nearly two years, so what were a few more weeks or months of waiting? Time and patience were everything.

Over the next several weeks, no updates arrived from Agnes. Finally, in late September 2011, Agnes messaged confirming that the household system in Taipei indeed had record of my sister's address. Was this the same sister and address that Tien had identified months earlier? Surely it was. Agnes referred to this individual as my *second* sister. I assumed that meant the second sister born to the family. I wondered about my other two sisters. Per my adoption contract, I was the fourth daughter born in the family, which meant I had two other siblings. Nevertheless, we were inching forward, and I gladly welcomed any news at all. Agnes cautioned me that everyone in Taiwan registered with the household system and had an address listed, but that did not guarantee that the individual registered lived at that particular address. In other words, we could not be certain my sister still lived at the address provided by the registration office. Despite her qualms, I felt beyond a shadow of a doubt that the person in question was my biological sister. It was an intuitive hunch. I ventured that Agnes did not want to get my hopes up only to have them dashed if the individual thought to be my sister was not. I could not blame her. She reported she would attempt contact with my sister as soon as possible, and I waited expectedly for that time.

In early October 2011, during the fall school break, my family and I took a hiatus and traveled to California. We stayed with some dear friends of ours, Joe and Grace, who lived within miles of the ocean. I shared with them how far we had come in the search for my birth family, and they were excited that things were progressing so well. One evening, Grace, who is Korean, was flipping through television stations, when she settled on a Korean drama called *Boys Over Flowers.* I was not particularly interested at first in watching, but as the show continued, I became so caught up in it that one episode turned into a marathon. Our husbands laughed at us, but I was hooked. In fact, when my family and I returned to Arizona, I continued to watch back-to-back episodes during the wee hours of the morning until I consumed the entire series. The show struck a chord with me and inspired an appreciation for my Asian roots that was altogether new. I thought about learning Mandarin and began listening to K-Pop and popular Taiwanese pop artists, like Jay Chou and Leehom Wang. I also began watching Taiwanese dramas, including *Meteor Shower* and *Single Princesses and Blind Dates*, as well as other Korean dramas, like *City Hunter*. I could not get enough of these shows.

I contemplated traveling to Taiwan, but did not tell anyone, including my husband. I did not want my decision to be questioned and knew Pat would be concerned about the expenditures, which annoyed me to no end. If I went, I would save the money I earned from work so that I could pay for the trip myself. I asked Tien if she would be traveling to Taiwan the following year and told her I intended to learn Mandarin whether or not we found my birth family. I was purposely exploring my cultural roots and longed to speak the language. I hated that my birth heritage was so foreign to me. Tien told me that she might travel to Taiwan in January 2012 to celebrate the Chinese New Year with her family as she did yearly. She also asked if Agnes at the agency in Taipei had given me my sister's address. She had not, nor had I thought to ask. That, of course, prompted me to write to Agnes immediately and ask for my sister's address. On October 21, 2011, Agnes wrote back apologizing that she could not provide an address due to privacy laws and would first need a release of information from my sister. She further informed me that the agency would wait a few more weeks for a response from my sister and if none were received, Agnes would personally visit my sister's home. I wanted to fast forward time. Could Agnes not just make the visit instead of waiting for a verbal reply? I wondered what delayed my sister's response to the agency's inquiries? Agnes signed off and stated, *"Let's just keep waiting. Hope we could have good news for you next time."* The waiting was painstaking. I told myself, *"Just sit tight."*

After Agnes' last message, I emailed Tien to advise her that the agency would not provide my sister's address or any other identifiable information until they had first received her permission. We were both frustrated, and Tien wrote, *"I don't understand why they cannot give out the information because you are her bio sibling???? Let us wait. I might try to call the registration office again and see..."* There it was again. *"Let us wait."* It was maddening knowing that we had such strong evidence of my sister's whereabouts, yet could do absolutely nothing except wait for Agnes to make direct contact with her. Again, we were so close. I could not just sit back and do nothing.

On November 1, 2011, I took a gigantic leap of faith and booked a flight to Taipei as well as a hotel, The Landis Taipei, in Taipei City. Although we had not yet made contact with my biological sister, I felt strongly that it was just a matter of time. I knew that Tien had already booked a flight for January 15, 2012, so I arranged for the same flight. I would travel to Taiwan with Tien and we would continue our search together. There was nothing stopping me now. I planned to stay a total of ten days. If we were unable to find my birth family, I would have at least visited the place of my birth and experienced its culture. I finally summoned the courage and told Pat I had booked a flight to Taipei.

"You did what?" Pat asked.

"I booked a flight to Taipei." He looked at me anxiously, skepticism etched across his brow. I knew my idea of a good deal was quite different from Pat's, but I did not care. I was disappointed that he doubted my decision to go to Taipei, but was not entirely surprised.

"Did you book a hotel, too?" Pat asked.

"Yes," I replied. "The Landis Taipei. It was one of the least expensive hotels. I got a really good deal, and I used money from my own checking account," I continued. I had opened my own account so that I would not have to constantly give all my receipts to Pat every time I bought something.

"What if you don't find your birth family?"

"It doesn't matter," I answered. "At least I'll have gone to the country of my birth and experienced what it's like to be there. I just want to connect to my roots no matter what." It would take Pat some time to come around, but I did not really give him a choice. Eventually he realized how important this trip was to me. When others began supporting my journey, he grew more optimistic. I knew that the trip would be worth it, and it was the right time. Everything appeared to be falling into place. I was really doing this! I had no idea how things would unfold in Taiwan, yet felt faithful that the trip would be one I would never ever forget. I was bubbling over with hope.

Tien and I then tentatively planned our visit to Taiwan. We scheduled our departure for January 15, 2012, from Seattle, Washington. I would return on the 26th. Tien recommended a guide who typically helped adoptive families while they were traveling in Taiwan to complete their adoption processes. Tien would be able to help to a certain extent during our trip, but needed to conduct business for her adoption agency as well. I was to develop a plan for my stay in Taipei and forward that to Tien so she could arrange the schedule for both of us. I hardly knew where to begin.

In the meantime, I received another message from Agnes at the agency in Taipei. *"There must be news of her reaching my sister!"* I thought to myself. On November 20, 2011, Agnes reported that she had visited the residence believed to be my sister's, but no one was home. She said neighbors confirmed someone lived at the address, but did not know if that person was my biological sister. Agnes stated she would find a different time to make another visit. She also asked how Tien was able to retrieve my sister's address previously and wanted to compare the two addresses. I thought privately, *"We should have done that before."* I was not sure if Agnes was distrustful of Tien and her sources, which were reliable, or if at this point she wanted Tien's help. Until now, Agnes and her team had conducted their search independently even though I had asked if Tien could assist. I wrote back to Agnes and explained that Tien had obtained her information from a registration office in Taipei, but was denied any further information because she was not a blood relative. I offered to put her in touch with Tien, but Agnes replied, *"It seems a little blurred about all this. But we now know we could check with Tien. We need to discuss this with my supervisor, and we will let you know if we need help."* And that was that. I hoped that Agnes would not wait too long to revisit the residence believed to be my sister's, but there was no way of knowing when this would occur.

The weeks passed by with no new updates. Thanksgiving arrived, and soon it would be Christmas. Another Christmas. December was an especially busy month as Tien and I prepared for our trip to Taiwan in January. I was still trying to arrange a seat next to Tien on our flight overseas, but for some reason, EVA Air, the airline I booked with, could not find a passenger named Mei-Na Tien. Strange. At that time, I was not very concerned, however, and put it aside. I was simultaneously strategizing a plan upon arrival to Taipei. My intention was to visit the registration office that Tien had contacted, show the clerk my adoption contract and Taiwan passport, and plead for their help in releasing the name and address of my sister. I did not know what province of Taipei this office was located and hoped that either Tien or the guide could drive me there and help with translation. I also wanted to sightsee, but did not know what to see or how I would get around the city. I began searching the Internet for top attractions around Taipei and made a list of places that looked interesting.

I had also begun taking Mandarin lessons in early November from a Taiwanese tutor named Shuchen. Shuchen was about as petite and bright as a garden fairy and always had an infectious smile on her face. I appreciated her warm personality and cheery spirit. She was excited about my trip and taught me conversational Mandarin in Pinyin initially so that I could at least speak a few phrases by the time my trip arrived. Each week, she provided a new lesson and made recordings so that I could practice speaking Mandarin at home. I barely had time to study between lessons due to work and family and was positive my Mandarin sounded just awful. Why was it so difficult to learn a new language? I wished for more time and energy to focus on my lessons, but was at least making efforts.

机会

Opportunity

11.

None of us knows what the next change is going to be, what
unexpected opportunity is just around the corner, waiting a few
months or a few years to change all the tenor of our lives.
~ Kathleen Norris

Tien and I continued to communicate back and forth frequently. With Christmas right around the corner, everyone was in full holiday mode, although that did not deter Tien and I from attending to our search. In fact, our efforts increased. Tien wrote to me on December 2, 2011, that she had made a few phone calls over the past week to arrange for my visit in Taiwan. A guide named Elaine would take me sightseeing for a fee of $500 over a period of four days. Elaine would drive her car and would also assist in helping to locate my sisters. Tien further reported that she made several other phone calls to different registration offices throughout Taipei City to gather more information about my sister. The officials at one office recommended that I write a letter identifying myself and providing details about my search ahead of time so they could contact my sister prior to our arrival. What a great idea! Perhaps this was the golden opportunity we had been waiting for that could change everything. Tien would write the letter in Mandarin with all the necessary Taiwanese paperwork required and forward it to me for my signature. She requested my date of birth and a copy of my Taiwan passport with the photo page, which I readily sent to her. Tien said she was quite busy with work at that time and that preparing the letter and paperwork would take at least a week. This sounded like the best plan yet. I only hoped that this letter would get past the scrutiny of the registration office.

After a few revisions, Tien sent me the finalized letter for my signature. Each revision required that I copy the new document, scan it, and send it back to Tien via email. I was to mail the letter directly to the registration office in Taipei. On December 12, 2011, my co-worker, Rayn, and I set out for the post office during our lunch break to mail the letter with a copy of my adoption contract and Taiwan passport. Rayn was a recreational therapist, and we co-facilitated several patient groups at the hospital. She was a huge support during my search, and we became good friends at the hospital.

It was wet, cold, and rainy outside. As Rayn and I approached the Phoenix post office, she said, "I hope there's not a long line!" I heartily concurred. Once we stepped inside, we were dismayed to find a long snaking line of people waiting to mail all manner of Christmas packages and letters. I began to worry that we would not have enough time to mail the package during our lunch break. Then Rayn noticed a self-service kiosk near the entrance of the post office. I hurried over before anyone else got the same idea. At the kiosk, I realized that I could not read the address label Tien had sent because it was in Mandarin. I needed to add the zip code, but how would I know what zip code was the correct one? What if I was unable to mail the package? My heart quickened, but thankfully, once I typed in where the package was going, a postage label appeared with the appropriate city and postage in a matter of seconds. Whew! We got the package off and were able to get back to work before our break was over. I prayed that not only the letter arrived safely into the hands of the right person, but that it led us straight to my sister in Taiwan.

奇迹

Miracle

12.

When you get into a tight place and everything goes against you, till it seems as though you could not hang on a minute longer, never give up then, for that is just the place and time that the tide will turn. ~ Harriet Beacher Stowe

It was a week before Christmas. I took a few days off to spend time with family and friends and was grateful that my one-hour work commute to Phoenix was temporarily put off. On the morning of Christmas Eve, I received greetings from Agnes in Taiwan wishing my family and I a Merry Christmas. There was no news of my sister. I shot her a quick email back wishing her the same and prayed again that the letter sent to Taipei would open doors. *We just needed one door.* Fortunately, the holiday bustle kept my mind on other things.

As with every Christmas, we were hosting some of our friends from California, Jane and Kevin, and their young daughter, Sierra. This was a holiday tradition that we enjoyed every year. On the Eve of Christmas, we threw a Christmas party and invited our friends, Dave and Kathy, and their two children, Jade and Mia. Jade was their adopted daughter from China and Mia, their biological daughter. Jade was two years old at the time of her adoption in 2008 and was now five. She was given the adoptive name Jade because a single jade necklace was found around her tiny neck after she was left abandoned. Perhaps it was the only thing her birth mother could give her. I was sure that one day Jade would understand the significance of that necklace and the love with which it was given.

The evening was full of catching up with our friends. I attempted to hide the exhaustion I felt from the ongoing demands of my job and running around here and there in preparation for the party. Our kitchen became a buzz of conversation and laughter as everyone mingled and loaded their plates full of holiday food and goodies. I felt overwhelmed by the houseful of people and noise and decided to steal away upstairs to our bedroom for a few minutes of quiet. I logged onto my computer to check for any new email messages. Earlier in the day, I had messaged Tien wishing her a Merry Christmas. Now, she had left a reply for me. Tien's email began, *"I have the greatest Christmas gift for you."* As I continued reading, I was stunned. Tien had found my oldest sister in Taiwan! Her name was Christina Huang. Tien reported, *"You have two older sisters and one older brother."* A brother? I thought that I had three biological sisters, but realized that my adoption contract merely stated that I was the fourth daughter. I assumed that my siblings were all female. Tien further reported that she had corresponded with Christina and told her we would be in Taipei in January. Here is what my sister initially wrote to Tien,

Dear Miss Tien,

I am Christina Huang, the elder sister of Marijane (Buck) Nguyen.

I just received letters from the local Household Registration Office today.

To my greatest pleasure that my youngest sister (黃筱玲) is now very well in USA and she will visit Taiwan early next year.

Though we family members missed for almost half century, like a broken kite line. Thank God, we finally find each other in our lifetime. Isn't it a miracle?

Actually my younger sister now lived in the old house. I moved to current place about eight years ago with my father. I'll inform her and my brother of the good news tomorrow.

It'll be very welcome to contact me when, if, Marijane is available. Please send my best wishes to Marijane. And I think we all are happy for the greatest gift of God, our reunion.

Merry Christmas and Happy New Year to all of you.

Christina Huang

Tien replied immediately and wrote,

Dear Christina,

I am so excited to hear from you. I have been helping Marijane since last year but never have any result.

We'll be in Taiwan on Jan. 16 by EVA airlines. If it is possible we can arrange a meeting on 16th night. I will send out this exciting news to Marijane and believe she will be very excited as well.

Your English is so well and believe the communication between you and her won't be a problem. One of my workers who has went to your old address but couldn't find any because BanCiao has changes a lot since 10 years ago.

Looking forward to meet you all.

Best wishes to all of you and God Bless!!
Tien

I stared at my computer screen, dazed, tears streaming down my face. The tides had finally turned. I let the news sink in. Tien had done it. We had done it. She had found my birth family! And my sister, Christina, remembered me! *Thank God, we finally find each other in our lifetime. Isn't it a miracle?* Indeed, it was a miracle. I was overjoyed that my sister wanted to meet me. I had feared that my birth family would not remember me or want to reunite and was unsure how old my siblings were at the time I was left for adoption. I hoped that the rest of the family also wanted to meet me. I noticed that Christina spoke and wrote in English far better than I had expected and thought perhaps Tien had translated her email, but Tien informed me that she had made no translations. I would not need a translator or guide after all. I ran downstairs as fast as I could to share the news with my family and friends. We celebrated together, thankful that my birth family had been found and that I would soon reunite with them halfway across the world. Whatever doubts Pat had previously about my trip to Taiwan completely disappeared. Tien was right. She had delivered the best Christmas gift ever that year.

天意（命运）

Fate

13.

Do not be afraid; our fate cannot be taken from us; it is a gift.
~ Dante Alighieri, *Inferno*

I was elated after reading Christina's email. The rest of Christmas Eve was a blur as I turned over and over in my mind what had transpired. We had finally found my birth family! All the waiting and detours were like a drop in the bucket. I wrote to Christina that night after everyone had retired. I stared at my computer screen blankly, not sure how to begin. What do I say? How should I introduce myself? It took several minutes to compose my thoughts and write that initial email to my sister. It went something like this,

> *Dear Christina,*
> *I am Marijane, your youngest sister, and I just received word from Tien that you contacted her. I am so happy to hear about you and that we have been able to find you! It is truly a miracle from God! I have been searching for my biological mother and father and any siblings for almost two years now. Tien has helped me with my search this whole time and has been very important in finding you. I never knew that I also had a brother. There is so much that I would like to tell you. I'm just so happy that you want to reunite! Tien and I will be leaving the States for Taiwan on January 15. We will arrive the morning of January 17 very early in the morning. I will be traveling by myself. My husband,*

Pat, and daughter will stay back. I've been married for 17 years now, and our daughter, Lexie, is 14-years old. We live in Chandler, Arizona, which is in the Western part of the U.S. just to the east of California. I am a music therapist and work at a psychiatric hospital. I love music and play the piano and guitar and sing a little. I'm wondering if anyone else in the family has musical ability?

I am very excited to come to Taiwan and meet with all of you! I have not been back to Taiwan since the time that I was adopted. I've been taking lessons in Mandarin Chinese, although I'm not very good at speaking fluently yet! I'm determined to learn how to speak Mandarin though.

I wish you a very merry Christmas, Christina! God bless you and your family! I am so grateful to be able to meet you soon! Thank you for wanting to meet me!

Marijane

I could barely get the words out fast enough once I started. An exclamation point punctuated the end of nearly every sentence I wrote. I was not even sure if there were exclamation points in Mandarin and whether my sister would recognize what they meant. Later, I learned that Christina suspected I was searching for the family. Her second email to Tien said,

Dear Miss Tien,

Thank you for your reply and we all are so excited about the meeting.

We might have just missed an arm's chance to get in touch last year. Our building guard ever received a call

*from the local police office about some relative looking
for things, however, when I tried to get the police officer
charged, there left no way to contact. Therefore we are
so lucky to have the dream come true now. And you are
an angel to help us together.*

*I ever majored in languages at the University. As not
quite using it in long years, and at my age, lots of words
can't remember. Still I'll do my best and we all look
forward to meeting you all.*

With my best wishes,
Christina

All that time had gone by, and as Christina said, we had apparently
just missed *an arm's chance to get in touch* the previous year. No matter,
I supposed that the timing was perfect and was meant to be as it turned
out. I also learned that Tien's helper in Taiwan had visited Christina's old
address in Bancaio all those months ago, the one listed on my adoption
contract where my second sister currently lived, but was unable to find
it because the province had changed so much. It was all a tangled web.

I received my first email from Christina a couple days following
Christmas. I could not wait to read it. On December 28, 2011, she wrote,

Dear Marijane,
*I'm so glad to hear from you and sorry for the delayed
answer, intermitted due to my setting a new computer
as to browse Internet better and faster.*

*I also have lots to say to you about things. But first, would
you please always try to understand and image what I
say, because I can't express well exactly what I want to
say in English. I think we can talk bilingually when meet
and very glad you've learned some mandarin which if
we stay along longer together, we'll both improve lots.*

Our reunited joy must be the everlasting wish of your biological mother (1928-1998) and father (1911-2008), May God bless them in heaven. And I'm also very thankful for your adopted parent for their love and the well care of you.

Actually we siblings had been a little bit alienated when we were very young maybe because our parents didn't get along very well at that time, which shadowed and made each of us an unhappy childhood, Yet, it enabled us be stronger and wiser about life too. We are very well and very close now.

Our brother, (8 years elder than me), has a son, 31 years, my sister (1 year younger than me) has a son at 28, and a daughter at 24. As for me, at 56, no children. Yet, I love everybody's children as my own and have donated for some children in Taiwan and in China, thankful to my husband's support.

We siblings seem all have kind of tendency on art and were good at painting and music when as a child. Yet we didn't go on the training especially.

In latest years, brother is keen and appreciated in photography. And sister work on designing, website etc.

I retired for over ten years. I ever did as a volunteer in a Chi-Gun association, a coach as well for a couple of years. Meanwhile I also took courses on literature and classic music, which I love and enjoy very much though I don't know much. Then I got realized that I'd too tight schedule and quitted to do volunteer in the last two to three years. Now I only keep few courses to be more free and for health's sake.

We are so proud of you for your versatile.

It was indeed something strange that I had unusual and very strong feeling to self-talk in English in mind in these two months, it just kept on coming up my mind and didn't clear what it was at all due to long years no using, which won't happen before. Now I understand it might [be] because you are searching and thinking of us especially during the time.

We can't but believe life is destined, and we are very lucky to have the blessing from God on our precious reunion.

I talk too long and thank for your patience and look forward to seeing you.

With my best wishes to you and your family and Tien.

Christina, and our other siblings

I was impressed that Christina's English was so good, much better than my Mandarin. I wondered what religion she and my family practiced because of her references to God and knew that Buddhism was the predominant religion in Taiwan. I sensed already that Christina was a gracious and kind soul, and I treasured her message. I now knew when my birthparents, our parents, had died. I was struck by her remark that our parent's everlasting wish was for our joyful reunion. They wanted us to reunite one day! I wondered if our father ever regretted taking me away from the family? If he did, I imagined he kept it to himself.

The missing pieces were gradually coming together. Christina was eleven years older than me and my other sister was ten years my senior. My brother was quite a bit older at age sixty-four, and I was now forty-five. I was looking forward to learning more about my other two siblings. I was fascinated by Christina's disclosure of experiencing an unusual inclination to renew her English just months before we found her when she had not thought of or spoken the language in years. Certainly, it was because I was thinking of the family so fervently. Ironically, I had begun learning Mandarin around the same time. The powers to be were undoubtedly at play. My sister also said that she studied languages at the university in Taipei. No wonder her English was so proficient despite the lack of usage over the years.

During the few weeks prior to my departure to Taiwan, Christina and I corresponded almost daily. In my next email, I told Christina about my adoption and parents,

Dear Christina,

It's so wonderful to hear from you! Your English is very, very good. Much better than my Mandarin. I will have to learn more Mandarin from you while I'm in Taiwan!

I was very sad to hear that our mother and father passed away. I had a feeling that was the case. When I found my adoption contract, I learned of their ages and knew that they would be much older. My adoptive mom never showed me my adoption papers, and I only found them after her death in 2008. My half-sister here found a box in my parent's attic, which contained all my adoption papers and a lot of other things about my adoption. I was 42-years old then and am now 45 years old. It was funny, but I remember my adoptive mom telling me as a child that I was part Vietnamese and Japanese. When I found my adoption papers and learned that my biological parents were both Chinese, I was very confused. It has all been a mystery. I'm so happy to have found you and our sister and brother! My adoptive father was in the United States Air Force. My adoptive mother was a registered nurse. They flew from Okinawa to Taipei to adopt me from The Family Planning Association of China, which no longer exists. We lived in Okinawa for a year or two before my father was transferred to the U.S. I grew up in a town called Bossier City in the State of Louisiana. It's in the southern part of the U.S. I attended a 4-year college and studied piano performance. I taught piano for many years and now work at Arizona State Hospital in Phoenix, Arizona. It's a psychiatric hospital. I use music therapy with the patients, but it is a hard job. I lived in California for many years and met and married my husband, Pat, there. We moved to Arizona 8 years ago. I would one day like to live in Taiwan for a time. I'm not sure how my husband or daughter would feel about that, but maybe one day. Our daughter is in the 8th grade, which is one year before high school in the U.S.

When you say that you began to self-talk in English, I began taking Mandarin lessons around the same time. I have only studied Mandarin for about a month and a half. I love the language! I think God has really been working. What are our brother and sister's names? I look forward to meeting all of you! I'm interested in learning more about Chi-Gun. I'm interested in meditation and tai chi, although I have never taken tai chi because of my work schedule.

Christina, would you mind if I share our story on a blog that I write? A blog is kind of like a journal that is posted on the Internet through a blogging website. I write on a blog site called Wordpress. You can Google it and see other blogs on this website. I have been writing about my search for all of you for a little over a year now. I have written all about my adoption as well and included many pictures.

I have to run off to work now. I work very far away from where we live, about an hour's distance. I am very

*excited to meet all of you soon. Have a very good day. I
feel so lucky and blessed to have found you!*

Love,
Marijane

I wanted to share the news that I was corresponding with my
biological sister in Taiwan on my blog, but felt it important to ask
Christina first before telling the world about my birth family. In her
next email, Christina said she had found my blog and had read some of
my posts. I was impressed she found it. My eyes grew wide as I read
her email.

Dear Marijane,

*I am very glad to know your blog and took some time to
find it on WordPress site.*

*Touched by your adoption story when I just glimpsed a
few of the journals. I think you are extremely excellent
at writing and the site is also beautifully designed. I'll
finish all later this night.*

*I saw the baby picture of you on exciting mood and all
memory comes back. When I was ten years old you were
born as a very beautiful and very adorable baby just
like the picture shown.*

*Father sent you away every day for the care of a
babysitter who lived near our home (which address I
think registered in your adoption paper). I and your
older sister (Amy) would go the babysitter's house to see
and play with you after school. Then all of a sudden we
couldn't find you because you were adopted, which at
our age could not understand.*

To my greatest sadness, mother was not informed of it ahead, and gone crazy of it and with pain in heart all her life. She wasn't well in physical and mental health at that time, which went along finance trouble and doubled the reason why you were adopted.

For so many years we still got vague memory of the baby image of you and we missed you all the time. Father said you were with Hong Kong parent when asked many times and he didn't seem clear about it either. I anyhow feel comfort that you've been better cared by your adopted parents. And I am happy for you, and we all are proud of you for your current success.

The Chi-Gun I've done is specially for exercising spine, in the other word, the central nervous system, which controls the whole work of a man's body. Therefore, it's a very strong and effective way to get healthy and energetic. It also involves the deep Chinese philosophy for life and soul. I can teach you if you would like to learn when there is chance later, which I think is of high possibility. After all you are young and have family and job's responsibility to do now

I'll tell Amy, your older sister, and John, your brother, about your blog, no matter whether they can understand all English or not. At least they can see your beautiful pictures at first.

Alas, I talk too much again

See you then.

Love,
Christina

My sister was named Amy and brother, John! I could now put a name to my other siblings. What struck me most about Christina's email was that I was taken for adoption without our mother's foreknowledge. I imagined the aftermath of despair I would have felt had my own daughter been removed from my care. My heart ached, and I felt compassion for our mother. I understood why I was placed for adoption and was deeply moved by Christina's story. My heart softened even more as I learned that Christina and Amy went to visit and play with me after school only to find me vanished one day. I wished that I could remember them; remember our brief time together. Perhaps it was better that I did not. I was not surprised to learn that there was financial hardship. Unfortunately, many children are placed for adoption in countries overseas for this very reason. Strangely, I found comfort in the thought that my sisters had not forgotten me and missed me long after I had gone. I finally knew that my birthmother had not wanted to surrender me and that it had caused tremendous emotional and physical pain. I was left barely able to catch my breath. Did our mother struggle with depression or some other illness? I did not want to probe at that time.

On December 30, 2011, Christina sent another email. What she shared was what I had longed to know and understand. Christina wrote,

Dear Marijane,

I've read through all your journals and truly understand what you had been put on to the situation about the cultural and racial dilemma. It must be natural summon for one to search the roots. The reconceive wouldn't be easy though. God is actually opening another door from the other hand.

We've had a long story for this life, because of this family, legendary enough, some sad, some pleasant and so much dramatic. If I were a good writer, I'd have created novels with this non-short-of materials. Amy is also good at writing as you do.

You resemble mother very much as what she looked when she was young. She was overwhelmingly beautiful then, though

she looked a bit different when after long term of hard time. Father was quite handsome. He was very strict and solemn, we all were scared of him when as a child. He just liked most fathers in a traditional Chinese society and showed his love unspokenly. Our parents seemed have got too much gifts from God and they might have had been jealous? As the victims of historical tragedy, Japanese invasion war and China communist war, they had suffered much when and after the moving from China to Taiwan. Fortunately, I'd been able to take care of them when they were old, which thankful to my husband's help and forgiveness.

Let go all the sadness about the split family and embrace the joy of our reunion. And I am so grateful for your having searched hard for us. It won't be possible if not so, because we didn't have any clue about you, no way to trace at all. I feel lucky enough not ever to change my registered address. You know, there is a very powerful household register system in Taiwan.

I had the same idea to prepare our parents' pictures for you when you come to Taiwan. Sorry, I don't have a scan machine at hand to send you now. It's a pity that we don't have many of the old time, especially of mom's, who burnt all early pictures when some quarrel happened with pa. And the conflict of parents was beyond our understanding and imagination as a child.

I know you've been busy around with work and family and hope it won't take you much time on our correspondence. And be sure to take care of yourself all the time. Be happy and healthy.

Love,
Christina

I marveled at the ability in which Christina wrote in a language she had not used in a while. I wondered if it was difficult for her to translate her thoughts to English. I began to paint a mental picture of what our parents were like. I am certain that I would have been afraid of our father as well and was grateful that Christina shared so much of our family history and circumstances at that time. It appeared there was much conflict, and my sisters also felt anguish because of it. In the end, Christina cared for our parents as they grew older. It was obvious she sacrificed in doing so. Christina said that our parents were victims of historical tragedy, including the Japanese invasion of China and the Chinese communist war. I knew she was referring to the Chinese Civil War. Our parents had fled China with the mass exodus to Taiwan in the early 1950's. It would appear they were escaping from Communist rule and political ideals they did not support and could be harmed had they stayed in China. How difficult that journey must have been and the years of adjustment following. I was deeply saddened that I would never meet my birthparents, but eager to meet my biological sisters and brother. Likewise, I could hardly wait to see the pictures of our parents Christina was preparing.

* * *

The year 2011 was swiftly coming to a close. On New Year's Eve, I met with my Taiwanese tutor, Shuchen, for another Mandarin lesson. I shared with her the incredible news that we had found my birth family, and a smile lit her face as bright as the noonday sun. I became more determined to learn as much Mandarin as I could before leaving for Taiwan, and she was just determined to help me be successful. That afternoon, Shuchen taught me a new phrase: *yǒu yuán* 有缘. When translated, it means, "have fate." She wrote out in Pinyin, *"Wǒmen yǒu yuán,"* 我们有缘, meaning, "We have fate." I could not think of another sentence more fitting.

桥梁

Bridge

14.

Sadly enough, the most painful goodbyes are the
ones that are left unsaid and never explained.
~ Jonathan Harnisch, *Freak*

Barber's *Adagio for Strings* swelled in the background,
each strain bled woefully into the next. I knew that I was
dreaming, but what I saw before me appeared so vivid, it
felt real. From out of the shadows a dark, ominous figure
emerged. Fear gripped me. The figure beckoned me
closer, and as I inched forward, I recognized the figure
as female. I strained to see her face, but it was hidden
behind an enormous hood, and the rest of her body was
cloaked beneath a long, gray robe the color of ash. I
continued to walk closer to the figure, holding my breath
with every step. As the music modulated to a major
mode, realization suddenly struck. The figure was my
birthmother. I don't know how I made the connection,
but deep inside I knew it to be true. The sobs came
uncontrollably. My birthmother slowly reached out to
me. She was slender and remained silhouetted by her
cloak. All I could see were her long, graceful fingers,
so elegant and beautiful. She drew me closer to her. The
fear dissipated as I felt the warmth of her embrace. She
told me, *"I never wanted to give you up. It was I who*
gave you the gift of music." I clung to her as she sought
to comfort me, her cheek pressed against mine. We did

not need words to express what we felt in that moment. As the music crescendoed I felt an ache inside of me that I had never experienced before grow, like a rip to my soul. The strings rose to a feverish pitch, and I thought that I would explode with all of the sorrow and joy that I felt simultaneously. The music gradually softened, and flowed into Mozart's *Serenade for Strings in B-flat.* The oboe and clarinet sang out their gentle refrain in perfect time. I could not stop crying. Then, I saw my adoptive mother just the way I remembered her as a child, happy, loving, before times grew dark. Her head was adorned with a nursing cap and she wore white. Her face glowed, and her smile was as bright as the waves of the sea. She looked down upon me with such love that it was almost more than I could bear. She did not speak, but I understood exactly what she was telling me. *"I'm okay! Don't worry about me anymore."* She wanted me to know my birthmother. She was bringing us together. She smiled down upon my birthmother and I embracing, nodding her approval. I did not want this moment to end. The music was changing again, soulfully winding down. My birthmother let go of her embrace, and I knew it was time for her to go. She released my hands and began to walk away. I longed to see her face, but it remained cloaked. Finally, she disappeared into the shadows. Swiftly, more images appeared, like bright lights or angels, and began gathering around my mother. The angels formed parallel lines and lifted her overhead. They were taking Mom away. I watched silently, tears flooding down my cheeks. The angels progressed slowly in time with the music towards an intricately adorned gate, golden and studded with pearls. I knew they were there to carry my mom to heaven. The gate opened. I watched as the angels carried her through. As the last few measures of music played out, the angels became smaller and smaller fading into the distance, and the

gate closed shut. I knew that my mothers were gone, but
not before each had said a final good-bye.

This dream haunted me for many days following the reconnection
to my sister, Christina, in Taiwan. It first occurred in the most unlikely
of places - during a music therapy workshop at Arizona State University
held just months after Mom passed away. My classmates and I had
recently graduated with our certifications in music therapy, and a
gathering of us came together to attend the workshop to learn The
Bonny Method of Guided Imagery and Music or GIM. We practiced
the techniques taught to us on one other, which involved guiding your
partner first into a deep, relaxed state to open the mind. We lay on the
floor, eyes closed, as our partners, or guides, kneeled behind us. Music
therapists trained in this method choose classical music sequences
that stimulate journeys of imagination. It is believed that the inherent
power of classical music evokes metaphoric levels of the psyche, which
promotes a whole new awareness and brings hidden or forgotten
material to the surface of the conscious (Bush, 1995). It is thought that
experiencing imagery in this way facilitates the integration of mental,
emotional, physical, and spiritual aspects of one's well-being (Bush,
1995). Although I was fully conscious of my surroundings and what was
happening, I had entered a dream-like state when the images occurred. I
was embarrassed that I could not control my sobbing as I underwent this
journey and hoped that my partner, David, was not completely freaked
out. One of the facilitators eventually came to his aid to help guide and
support me. When the journey ended, I opened my eyes to see David,
perhaps a little intimidated by what had occurred. I tried to see past
his smile to determine what he was really thinking. Was he glad the
whole thing was over? Did he think I was a weirdo? I could not tell. If
anything, neither one of us expected such an intense experience, as this
was only the first level of the Bonny Method training. When everyone
had completed their journeys, our facilitators handed out pieces of blank
paper, crayons, and colored pencils and instructed us to draw mandalas
to help process what we had experienced. I was not sure how to begin.
I felt disjointed, and it was difficult for me to concentrate. I wanted
time alone to go over again what I had experienced. No one else had

undergone a journey in any way close to mine. The facilitators said that it was not uncommon for clients to connect with loved ones who had passed on in their practice and gently encouraged me to believe what I had experienced was in fact very real. I was skeptical initially thinking I was only grieving the loss of my mom. I realized later that I did not have to question my experience and accepted that my mothers came to me through some spiritual channel to convey something vitally important. The images came back when Christina and I connected. I believed this happened because of what I had learned about my birthmother - that it was not her wish to lose me to adoption and that it had occurred without her knowledge and consent. Little did I know back in 2008 that what my birthmother revealed to me in that dreamlike state was true. Now, I agonized over the thought that my birthmother never recovered from her loss, my relinquishment. I thought about her often as I began my preparations for the trip to Taiwan, which was right around the corner. I would never meet my birthmother yet felt strongly that Christina was a bridge, a conduit to her. I wondered what our mother would say to me had she lived to see our reunion. I wondered how much more conflict between our mother and father occurred and in the family because of this twist.

It has been said that the most painful goodbyes are the ones that are left unsaid and never explained. Perhaps that is why I experienced the dream I had of my birthmother and adoptive mother. So many things were left unsaid and unexplained. My birthmother never had the chance to say good-bye to me. I was taken away from her in such a way that she never fully recuperated according to Christina. My adoptive mother and I never had the chance to say good-bye because of an illness that seized her memory. The secrets she and my father kept about my past lay buried in an attic for years, forgotten. Now it was time to get ready for a new journey - a journey back to my origins, to my heritage. The following weeks were full of preparations for my trip to Taiwan. My birth family was waiting for me on the other side of the world. I was going home.

巧合

Coincidence

15.

Do you think the universe fights for souls to be together? Some
things are too strange and strong to be coincidences.
~ Emery Allen

EVA Airlines could still not find Tien on the flight I booked to
Taipei. I spoke to the customer service representative yet again.

"Yes, T-I-E-N. Mei-Na. That's right," I said to the representative.
Minutes went by.

"Ma'am, there is no passenger with that name booked on this flight,"
he finally answered. How could that be? How was I to arrange a seat next
to Tien if they could not even find her? I was scheduled to leave from
Seattle on January 16, 2012, for Taiwan, the same date Tien informed
me she would be leaving. I was frustrated and confused after multiple
attempts to locate Tien on the passenger list. I emailed Tien with my
flight information. She wrote back, *"This flight arrives two days later.*
We are on two different flights. Oh no. Can you change it?" I had booked
the wrong flight! In my haste to arrange flights, I had not calculated the
time difference. There was still time though; it was only the first week
of January. I was able to rebook my flight at minimal cost, although Tien
and I would not be able to sit next to each other. At least we would be
on the same flight. I would depart from LAX International Airport in
Los Angeles on January 15, 2012, and fly to Seattle where I would meet
Tien. We would then leave Seattle Tacoma International Airport at 1:00
am and arrive at Taiwan Taoyuan International Airport the morning of
January 17th around 6:20 am. It appeared to be a two-day trek to Taiwan,

but with time zone differences, the flight was approximately twelve to thirteen hours.

My sister, Christina, and I continued to send emails to one another up until the day I left. She sent me a colorful calendar with photographs of Taiwan. The pictures gave me a first glimpse of Taiwan's beautiful landscape - picturesque orange and red sunsets hovering the ocean, luscious green peaks and valleys, rivers and misty waterfalls flowing over red clay rocks. I wished that I could read Mandarin so I knew where in Taiwan the photographs had been taken. Christina and I also Skyped, although she had her web cam turned off during our conversation so I could not see her face. I did not say anything, but wondered if she knew her camera was off. I thought maybe she wanted to stay private until we met in person. No matter, it was good to hear her voice and talk to her, despite my disappointment in not being able to see her face to face. One of the emails Christina sent before I left was especially interesting. She said,

> *Dear Marijane:*
>
> *I was very glad to chat with you on skype yesterday, though not much. There are always chance next time.*
>
> *I went to see Amy's Mother-in-law who is right-side paralyzed with clear consciousness. I told her the story how you are back. She cried with tears. Though she couldn't speak I could see from her face that she was so glad and felt comfort for us. She is very kind to us so we regard her as a mother.*
>
> *Amy' sister-in-law (her husband's sister) approaches about ancient Chinese zodiac and Bagua Astrology.... She said you are a zodiac horse, who would always run far away from birth home. Coincidence happens.*

Each time Christina shared something new related to our family or about my past, I was captivated. I was touched that Amy's mother-n-law cried over our reunion, and wondered how she came to be paralyzed. I prayed that God would restore her to good health. I continued to create a mental picture of my family – what they looked like and what their personalities were like based upon what Christina passed on to me. I was also intrigued by what Amy's sister-n-law said about my Chinese horoscope, and knew that I was a Horse according to my birth year, but had never paid much attention to Chinese astrology. I learned that the *bāguà*, 八卦, literally means "eight symbols." The symbols are part of a very complex system of philosophical Chinese beliefs rooted in Taoism. I have always been mystified by astrology and was curious about what Amy's sister-n-law said - that I would always run far away from my birth home. Was it a strange coincidence that I would be separated from my birth country and family for four decades only to return in the most inexplicable way? It was more than a coincidence, I thought. It had been meant to be.

In the meantime, Christina began asking what I most wanted to see in Taiwan and suggested several attractions including Sansha Old Street, Sansha Ancestral Temple, Yingge Ceramics Museum, and Yingge Old Street. She attached colorful photos of each site. The pictures were impressive and displayed small quaint shops with red brick pillars and handsomely carved gables, life-size stone statues of ancient Chinese figures, beautiful white ceramic teapots streaked with cerulean, and imposing ceramic horses the colors of caramel, cream, and amber. Christina also wanted to take me to Hualien, a city located in east Taiwan nestled by the Pacific Ocean. I was delighted to receive the pictures and thought that going anywhere with my sisters would be wonderful.

Tien and I also stayed in touch as we counted down the days to our trip. A few days before our departure, I received an email from her informing me that news reporters from Taipei were interested in reporting on the story of my reunion with my birth family. Tien thought our story would help others better understand international adoption and send a positive message about such adoptions, which were viewed unfavorably by the Taiwanese. I quickly agreed to the interview, but asked that Tien speak to Christina and Amy to see how they felt about it. Christina soon after wrote to me and said she was shocked when a reporter contacted her and intended to come by her home for an interview. Although the reporter was polite and said he would protect her privacy, Christina was taken by surprise and declined to participate in the interview, believing that news reporters in Taiwan had become like the paparazzi. Tien continued to press for an interview to include my sisters suggesting a phone interview as an alternative to limit their visibility, but I knew Christina would oppose any contact with the press. I told Tien so, and it was decided that I would participate in the interview alone. Tien would make the arrangements for a date and time with the reporters. I was so excited about our reunion that I wanted to share this extraordinary event with the whole world, but also wanted to respect Christina's wish for privacy.

One week before our trip, Christina wrote that everyone in Taiwan was busy getting ready for the Lunar New Year or Chinese New Year. She had said previously that the Eve of the Lunar New Year fell on January 22, 2012, and on that date families would join together for a special dinner following Chinese tradition. I thought, how ironic that I would be reuniting with my birth family during the Lunar New Year celebration. Christina hoped that though Amy customarily joined her husband's family for this occasion, we could all celebrate together this year. It would be the first time that I ever celebrated Chinese New Year, as I had never observed the holiday in the States. I began to feel nervous, wondering how the other members of our family felt about me. Did they want to me meet me or rather felt obligated? That was surely the last thing I wanted. Would we be able to communicate? I did not speak Mandarin, and although Christina spoke proficient English, what about the rest of the family? Would there be awkward silences across the dinner table? I put my worries aside and focused on how fortunate I was. I placed a countdown calendar on my blog so that I could count down the days with my followers.

The rest of the week went by quickly. I spent the last few days before my trip searching for gifts for my family. I fretted over what to purchase, things small enough to fit in my luggage, yet memorable. Tien recommended buying gifts unique to Arizona to give my family an impression of the state I lived in. I went to our farmer's market and found small custom prints of native Arizona flowers and the Grand

Canyon and picked up locally harvested jars of honey and mini prickly pear cactus jellies. I visited Sharpley's West, in downtown Chandler, a gift store with distinguished gifts from Arizona and bought chocolate bars wrapped in pictures of the Old West, desert aloe soaps, decorative pens, and other little trinkets. I carefully stowed the gifts I selected in my suitcase, hoping they would arrive in Taipei undamaged.

The day of my departure was soon approaching, and Christina kept in close contact informing me of weather changes, advising me to bring warm clothing, medicines for influenza and possible headaches, and a coat, hat, scarf, and gloves for the cool, windy weather. She also suggested I bring a swimsuit for the hot springs we would visit in Hualien. We would visit Taroko National Park on the way to Hualien, and Christina had hired a driver to take us from the park to Hualien. We would leave on a train the second day after my arrival. I was impressed by all the arrangements that Christina had made and grateful for her kindness. Her parting words to me that evening were, *"It's about time you come to Taiwan. I hope you have very happy journey and have sweet dreams."* I would leave tomorrow evening for Seattle and then onward to Taiwan in the wee hours of the morning.

In bed that night and unable to sleep, I was amped up and slightly worried about flying. I was not a good traveler and prone to motion sickness. There were several flights where I did not take Dramamine soon enough and was consequently left miserable for days afterward. I counted my thoughts as they flit across my mind like pebbles strewn across a stream. I believed that the universe, as they say, had fought to bring my sisters and I together – three souls that would soon be reunited. And, I was fairly certain that likewise, the universe had brought Tien into my life for this very moment.

想起

Remember

16.

There's nowhere you can be that isn't where you're meant to be.
~ John Lennon

I woke up the next morning full of excitement, nerves, and worry all meshed into one giant ball of emotions. I did not sleep well the night before, fretting over last minute errands and packing that needed to be finished before we left for the airport. My flight was scheduled to leave from Phoenix at 2:30 pm for Seattle. I felt a rush of adrenaline as I ran out to buy little things like eye drops, giftwrap, and travel size toiletries. Why had I procrastinated? When I arrived back home, Lexie was upstairs painting her nails, while Pat, was watching football. The banter of sports commentators droned on in the background as they made predictions about the upcoming Patriots and Broncos game. It was a big game, but I would miss it while in flight. I worried about Lexie and Pat and how they would fair while I was gone. Pat would drive Lexie to and from school as well as to all her extracurricular activities - voice and dance lessons. I finished packing, leaving a little room for things I would buy in Taiwan. Despite my attempts to pack frugally, my suitcase and backpack weighed a ton.

At last it was time to leave for the airport. Pat loaded my luggage into the back of our car, and we all piled in. I could not shake my nerves and felt the anxiety increase as I worried about getting airsick. I had placed a small patch of scopolamine behind my ear the night before and prayed that it would not fail. I would hate to arrive in Taiwan nauseated. Once at the airport, I kissed Pat and Lexie good-bye and gave Lexie an especially big hug.

"Have a great time, Mommy! I love you!" she said affectionately.

I love you too, little Twitter," I replied, planting a giant kiss on the top of her head. I hated saying good-bye.

"Skype us when you get to your hotel," Pat reminded me.

"I will," I answered. They waved good-bye and watched me walk into the terminal, bags in tow. I stepped up to the counter to check in, but could not get my boarding pass to print. A kindly airline representative sauntered over to assist.

"Are you traveling to Taiwan?" she chirped.

"Yes, I am," I replied.

"I like your airport."

Her remark struck me as odd. *My* airport? She assumed that I was from Taiwan, that I lived there. I felt proud that she thought I was a native.

"Actually, I've never been to Taiwan. This will be my first time there."

"Oh!" she exclaimed. The airport there is very big, like a huge warehouse." She then asked why I was traveling to Taiwan. I explained briefly that I was adopted and going to see my birth family for the first time since my adoption.

"Oh, how wonderful!" she said. We conversed a little more. "How many people are in your birth family? She asked.

"Well, I have two older sisters and an older brother, but my birth parents passed away," I told her.

The rep sympathized and said, "Well at least you have siblings to meet."

She was friendly and like so many others I told about my story, astonished that I was able to find my birth family and reconnect with them. I was distracted by my own thoughts, however, introspective and a little detached. I was glad when our conversation ended and headed up the escalator to the security checkpoint. As I looked around, I noticed how empty the airport was. No long waits in line for either check-in or security. I hurried to my gate. Once I sat down, I immediately grabbed my backpack so I could retrieve my laptop and start blogging. The sharp voices overhead of airline workers announcing boarding times and loud hum of conversation drowned out as I put my headphones on and cranked up the music. The second movement of Bach's double violin concerto eased away my anxiety, and I settled back into my seat to begin writing.

* * *

I arrived in Seattle just shy of 5:00 pm. The flight was smooth, no unexpected bumps or motion sickness, along the way. It would be approximately eight hours before Tien arrived. I grabbed a shrimp salad and some chamomile tea, balking at the nine dollars it cost to purchase my salad. The hours ticked by ever so slowly, but I was so amped and eager to meet Tien, my miracle worker, that it made the wait worthwhile. Though we had exchanged hundreds of emails over the span of three years, we had never met in person. When she arrived, I recognized her immediately. She looked just like the picture she had sent, warm eyes, big affectionate smile, robust. She was animated, and I was immediately encouraged. Tien wrapped me into a giant hug, and we talked like two friends who had known each other our whole lives as we waited to board our plane. There were no words to adequately thank Tien for all she had done to make my reunion possible. She had carried me through, even when I had mistakenly believed she had forgotten me. Nevertheless, I attempted to tell her how grateful I was that she never gave up nor doubted that we would find my family. She smiled humbly, and with a wave of her hand, gestured as though it were nothing.

It was now 12:30 am and time to board. Butterflies danced wildly in my stomach as Tien and I lined up with all the other passengers. The plane was massive boasting an upper and lower deck, triple seating expanded across two narrow aisles. Tien and I found our way to the upper deck and to our seats. Unfortunately, we were not able to sit next to each other due to my blunder in booking flights months before. She told me not to hesitate to get her if I needed anything. I thought I should try to sleep, but was not in the least bit sleepy. I knew I needed to at least rest my mind after such a full day and eased back into my seat next to the window. Once airborne, the EVA flight attendants began serving a meal. It was 1:30 in the morning. I was not particularly hungry and picked at my food. Passengers were starting to doze off, except for the woman sitting to my left. Katie and her husband, the passenger to her left, were Taiwanese and traveling back home to Taipei. Katie wore thick black glasses and had a cherub-like face, her short dark hair was thick and pulled back loosely. She chattered on about all manner of things, most of which I do not remember. Upon learning that it was my first trip to Taiwan, she enthusiastically dispensed loads of advice that I would certainly not retain. Katie leaned in so close to me that her glasses almost clipped the side of my face. Even worse, she continued to poke my left sore arm, the one that had just been vaccinated, with her elbow as she rattled on. I finally had to interrupt Katie and tell her kindly that I was sleepy and wanted to rest before landing in Taipei. She took the hint and rather reluctantly turned away as I rested my head against the seatback, closing my bleary eyes. It was very quiet on the upper deck, no crying children, or loud boisterous passengers. I kicked off my shoes, and the whirr of engine noise soon lulled me into a fitful sleep.

I slept in bouts until about two hours before our arrival, the flight attendants again served another full meal. *What bizarre times to eat,"* I thought, but enjoyed the hot, jasmine scented towels the attendants provided afterwards. The cabin came to life as we made our final descent into Taipei. Flight attendants scurried about in preparation for landing, and Katie once again took to lively conversation. I peered out the window at Taoyuen City beneath us. It was a beautiful sight. The morning was still dark, and specks of lights from below shimmered like a thousand tiny lanterns, snaking around the gentle curves of the highway. As we approached Taoyuen International Airport, I could barely stay in my seat. My sisters awaited our arrival and had arranged to take me to my hotel. A big smile as broad as the Golden Gate Bridge stretched across my face as we taxied down the runway.

Tien and I disembarked and headed directly to the currency window to exchange our American dollars. She set off at a brisk pace, and it felt good to stretch my legs and move about after our long flight. *"The American dollar is down,"* Tien remarked, and I made a mental note of it. I was never very good at understanding currency exchange rates. Too much math. I would figure it out later.

The airport was large and contemporary with shiny white walls, high ceilings, and recessed lighting. I was glad that Tien was my guide and knew the appropriate checkpoints. Even more, Tien made me feel secure in a world that was so new to me. Her spirit ignited mine and kept me going. We filled out arrival cards and commenced to the arrival area for clearance. I stepped up to one of the windows and handed the officer my card. He looked it over then turned to me asking something in Mandarin. Tien stepped in to help, and I wished more than anything that I could speak Mandarin.

It seemed to take forever to complete the necessary steps before reaching baggage claim even though the lines moved rather quickly. The sound of Mandarin was everywhere, and I strained to understand even one word. It sounded foreign and unintelligible. There must have been a time in my life when the language was familiar. I looked around me. In the past, I had been extremely uncomfortable around other Asians and distanced myself from them. But now I took pride in standing among so many other Taiwanese.

Tien kept us moving and finally led the way downstairs to baggage claim where she picked up a large cart to put our luggage on. We wound our way through the throngs of people to the airport lobby, and I eagerly searched the crowds for my sisters. Across the lobby, I spotted a woman wearing a bright orange jacket like the one Christina described she would be wearing. She and the woman next to her were holding a sign that said, *"Welcome Marijane"* in big blue letters as they watched the influx of passersby. *"I found them!"* I shouted to Tien, and we quickened our pace. There were my sisters. *"Oh my gosh, my sisters are here!"* Amy, my second sister, sported a short bob hairstyle. She wore black-framed bedazzled glasses and a black leather jacket with a fur collar. Christina also had very short hair and wore glasses. A bright burgundy scarf was neatly wrapped around her neck. They both had similarly shaped round faces and were smiling warmly at us as Tien and I made our way toward them. I noticed that we were all nearly the same height. I embraced both of my sisters and introduced them to Tien. My sisters were unbelievably welcoming. We were all smiles and laughter. Christina's English was again far better than I had anticipated. She brought a little hand held electronic device that translated Mandarin to English and occasionally looked up a word, her fingers typing at the tiny keyboard. We talked about the flight over, and my sisters asked if

I was tired. I was not tired at all, but rather exhilarated. I supposed that I was running on adrenalin.

We continued to chat in the airport lobby then Christina and Amy showered me with gifts - little Taiwanese desserts and candies, a thermos for hot water, a knife for cutting fruit, and a hand phone, as they called it. Christina also gave me black and white photographs of our parents, three pictures of Pa, two as a young man, and the other taken when he was much older. She had made a disc of several more photographs of Pa and handed it to me. I could not believe that I was staring at the faces of my birthparents. I held the pictures in my hand and studied them. Pa was very handsome. His eyes were difficult to read, impassive and stern, yet large and attractive. He had a square jaw, and the bridge of his nose I recognized as my own. He was much older in another photo, perhaps in his seventies or eighties, and looked frail, as though life had humbled him. His eyes appeared hazy. I stared at the single photo of Ma, our mother, for several minutes searching her face for any mark of resemblance. She was not smiling and wore what looked like a thick, black shirt with a stiff Mandarin collar. Her hair was short and coiffed as in the style of older women. Her eyes were soft and turned down ever so slightly in the outer corners. She had a round face, and I thought there to be a hint of pain behind her eyes. They were sad eyes. I wondered what she was thinking when the photograph was taken and thought her to be in her late forties or fifties at the time. I noticed that my sisters also had beautiful round faces very similar to Ma's. Christina and Amy watched silently, patiently as I regarded each photograph.

Amy then leaned over to Christina and told her something in Mandarin, breaking the silence.

Christina translated, "She thinks you resemble our mother."

Amy looked intently into my eyes and continued in her best English, "When you were baby, I held you in my arms." She motioned with her arms as though cradling a baby, her voice soft and strong.

"I wasn't sure if you and Christina would remember me," I said. "I wasn't sure how old you were when I was placed for adoption." Christina translated this for Amy, and Amy nodded her head.

"We always remember you. We never forget," replied Amy, smiling. I let her words resonate in my mind. *We always remember you.* I was sure that with the passage of time those memories must have faded, and yet my sisters never completely forgot.

Christina turned to me and showed me how to use the hand phone. She flipped screens and pointed out her phone number as well as Amy's. It was Christina's personal cell phone. She gave it to me so we could call each other while I was in Taiwan. With that, we all agreed that we should be on our way. Tien departed, hugging each one of us before leaving to meet her father. I was left alone with Christina and Amy who guided me outside so that we could catch a taxi to my hotel; neither of my sisters ever learned to drive. The drive would be nearly an hour.

We stepped into a queue of other travelers lined up at the curb awaiting taxis to transport them to their destinations. The sun had now risen, and I shivered as the cool morning air chilled me. We watched as one taxi after another pulled up then pulled away with a new crew of passengers. While we waited for a taxi, my sisters and I had time to talk and get more acquainted. Christina asked how my search for them started and how I was able to find them. I explained that it all began when I found my adoption papers. I told them how curious I became when I learned that my mother's story was so different from the information on my adoption contract – that our mother and father, Ma and Pa, were not Japanese or Vietnamese as my parents had told me, but were originally from China. I explained that I became extremely curious about my origins and that I wanted to find out about my birth family. I hoped all the while that my sisters understood what I was trying to say. They shook their heads as if they did.

At last, it was our turn to get into a taxi. My sisters and I hopped into the backseat, and Christina told the taxi driver where we needed to go. I looked out the window as we merged onto the highway into heavy traffic, trying to absorb Taiwan. Tall dingy buildings stood out against the gray sky. Every once in a while, a Buddhist temple off in the distance came into view, its golden spires reaching up toward the heavens. My sisters encouraged me to sleep, but I was not tired in the very least. I kept glancing at Amy and Christina straining to see any resemblance among the three of us. I thought Amy and Christina looked very much alike right down to their mannerisms. They were only one year apart in age, and their affection for each other was obvious. They seemed to communicate without saying a word, as though they were able to read each other's thoughts. I did not initially think that I looked like either Amy or Christina as much as they resembled each other, but I noticed that Amy and I had similar tastes in clothing. Both of my sisters seemed so youthful. It was hard to believe they were ten and eleven years my senior. They were affectionate and kind towards me, and I felt almost instantly that I was being cared for in the way a mother cares for her children. It felt warm and protective. How could they be so kind and generous? Although I was their younger sister, I was practically a stranger. It was almost too good to be true.

We talked the entire way to my hotel, asking questions, nodding and shaking our heads. We had so much to catch up on! Finally, we arrived at my hotel, and Christina and Amy escorted me into the lobby. The hotel was beautifully decorated in the style of French art deco. A spray of tall, red flowers punctuated with spruce in tall, slender vases welcomed hotel guests. Behind a console table, two large mahogany desks fitted with computers sat in the reception area. Taupe-colored curtains and white sheers swept across the back wall. I walked up to one of the desks where an attendant sat in a camel-colored leather chair. He rose when I approached the desk and greeted me in Mandarin with a warm smile. I explained sheepishly that I did not speak Mandarin. "Oh, welcome to the Landis Taipei!" the attendant replied. After confirming my registration, he handed me a key, and Christina and Amy accompanied me to my room to make sure I settled in okay. After they inspected my room, we discussed plans for dinner. It was still very early in the morning, and they wanted to give me time to rest. Christina suggested we talk later that afternoon to see how I was feeling. If I were not too tired, we would meet for dinner. No sooner had they left my room, I heard a knock at my door. It was my sisters. Christina extended a handful of money to me- $6000 NT dollars, or New Taiwan dollars, which was well over $100 American dollars.

"Money for spending and for busboy," Christina said.

"No, no I can't accept this!" I replied, but my sisters insisted that I keep the money. I thanked them, but felt guilty and did not want them to feel obligated to give me money.

"We call you later. Get some rest," my sisters chimed as I closed the door behind them.

My hotel room was very small, but comfortable. The queen-sized bed took up the majority of the room. It was made up in white linens and a white down comforter, and two nightstands stood on either side. A handsome desk, armoire and television, and a couple of armchairs were also provided. I made myself a cup of tea to warm up and peered outside my window. My room was on an upper floor, and I had a broad view of Taipei's bustling business and entertainment district. Tall gray and brown buildings surrounded the hotel on every block, air conditioning units hung from the windows, and scores of motor scooters lined the curbs. There was a McDonalds right across the street. I began unpacking my suitcase, putting clothing away in drawers and hanging shirts and sweaters in the closet. I laid on my bed, but itched to go out and explore. I felt awkward because of my inability to speak Mandarin and wondered if the attendant at the front desk thought it strange that I only spoke English. The staff were all young, friendly, and proficient in English. I was sure that they spoke the language to many American tourists, but I did not look like the typical American.

I sat on my bed, got my computer out and skyped Pat and Lexie. They were happy I made it safely to Taipei. I told them about my morning with my sisters and showed them the pictures Christina had given me of Ma and Pa.

"You look more like your father," said Pat. I actually agreed with him. I was relieved that Lexie seemed to be doing fine.

"I love you, Mommy," she said as we ended our call.

"Love you, too, sweetie!" I answered.

After our conversation, I could not decide whether to go out or stay in the hotel and relax until dinnertime. I decided to chill in my hotel room a bit to rest and write in my journal. How was I to even begin to write about such an exciting day? It felt like a dream. I decided to put it aside until after I met for dinner with Christina and Amy. Instead, I organized the gifts for my family, taking each one from my suitcase and carefully placing them in gift bags topped with colorful tissue paper. I took out the photo album that I made for Christina and Amy with pictures of my childhood, my parents, and Pat and Lexie. I also placed my adoption contract in the scrapbook. I slowly thumbed through the album, looking at all the pictures I had assembled. It was just a small representation of my life and what it was like growing up in America. I hoped they liked the album.

I went downstairs and explored the hotel. There was a lovely bakery to the right of the front lobby. Hotel guests browsed the bakery, gazing at the pretty glass displays of sweet breads, tarts, tiny desserts, and cakes. I bought a Napoleon, a French pastry with layers of light flaky crust and pastry cream filling. I had a college friend who loved Napoleons and was reminded of him. As I explored, I discovered that there were two different restaurants and a large piano bar. I stepped outside, ready to explore the area. It was muggy, and rainy out, typical of Taiwan's winter months. The streets were mostly quiet, and many of the shops were closed in observance of the Lunar Chinese New Year. The Zhongshan Elementary School MRT Station, or train station, was minutes away from the hotel, and there was a Starbuck's right down the street. I strode into a boutique to look at the clothing and shoes. A pair of flip-flops caught my eye, but I decided to wait and look at some other shops before purchasing anything. After walking a few blocks more, I turned back towards the hotel.

Once back in my hotel room, I turned on the television and flipped through multiple stations. Of course, I could not understand anything, but I liked listening to others speaking Mandarin. Before I knew it, I fell asleep. I was awoken later by the sound of Christina's handphone ringing. I reached over to the nightstand and picked up the phone.

"Hello?" I answered.

"Hello, Marijane. It's Christina. How are you feeling?" We spoke for several minutes and I told Christina that I felt well and was very excited to have dinner with her and Amy. That evening, Christina and Amy arrived in a taxi to take me out to dinner. They took taxis everywhere they went. I met my sisters' downstairs in the lobby. They had brought more gifts - oranges, fresh grapes, and cookies. I had also brought down gifts to give to each of them, as well as the photo album. I could not decide whether to give them all their gifts at one time or wait until the Lunar New Year's Eve, but finally decided to give a few gifts that evening.

The taxi ride to the restaurant was short, and we arrived at the restaurant in no time. We were shown downstairs, and within twenty minutes the restaurant was completely packed. I saw a few Americans sitting at tables on the other side of the room. I pulled the photo album out and began to show it to Christina and Amy, but put it away so we could order our food. Amy ordered for us, and we were soon served hot green tea. Our first entrée came out quickly - tofu and vegetables, followed by pig kidney, Chinese broccoli and other vegetables, rice, and a seafood dish. The food was steamy hot, fresh, and delicious. The only entrée I did not like was a brownish plant-like food that looked like squid or octopus and had a weird, slimy texture. I learned later that it was sea cucumber. I made sure to steer clear of sea cucumber the remainder of my trip. For dessert, we were served little squares of sticky rice rolled in peanut crumbs. It had a mushy texture and was quite yummy. Amy watched my face as I tasted my dessert and smiled at me reaction. My sisters used their chopsticks with ease while I struggled to coordinate mine. I was glad the rice was sticky. Amy told me again how much I looked like our mother, and I felt flattered that I resembled her. She and Christina thought the shape of my face resembled our Uncle, and Christina showed me a picture of him and his wife early in their marriage. Uncle's wife was gorgeous. I learned later that she died soon after their marriage. I asked Christina more about Pa and our brother, John.

"Father was in Army for a long time and later worked for the government," Christina said. I learned that Christina and Amy attended university, and Christina studied English and linguistics.

"I learn other languages easily," she explained.

"She speaks four different languages!" Amy exclaimed. Christina told me that Amy was a web designer and worked from home. Christina continued and said she had gone back to school for a higher degree when Pa fell and became very ill afterward.

"I returned to Taiwan to take care of him and never finished," she said. I learned that John owned a business and lived in Tainan, a southern region of Taiwan. He was married, but now single, and had one son.

"When you were born," Christina explained, "John was busy with entrance exams for university."

"Oh," I said nodding my head. I assumed that John was not at home often at the time of my birth. I blinked a couple of times, distracted by my contact lenses. My vision had become incredibly blurry, and I was having great difficulty seeing clearly. Whenever my sisters leaned in towards me as we talked, everything got fuzzy. I thought it to be a side effect of the motion sickness medicine I was taking and feared that I looked cross-eyed. *"Great,"* I thought to myself. *"My sisters probably think there's something wrong with my eyes."* It was extremely annoying and obscured my ability to focus clearly. Despite my crossed eyes, I was so happy to spend time with my sisters.

After dinner, we returned to my hotel. Christina and Amy accompanied me upstairs to my room, and I again brought out the photo album. I believed that they preferred to look at the album privately. They oohed and aahed over my baby pictures and told me I looked like a celebrity in my seventh-grade school photo.

"Did you have lots of dates?" they ask me laughing.

"No! Not at all!" I told them. "Quite the opposite." We came to the photographs of my parents. They studied the pictures of my mom and dad, and Christina remarked that my dad looked very much like Pa. I agreed. They were both very handsome and shared similar traits, like a receding hairline and military pasts that gave them an appearance of authority.

After looking at the photo album, my sisters departed, but not before encouraging me to eat the fruit they brought and get some sleep. We made tentative plans to have lunch together with Tien the next day after my interview with a local reporter in the morning. I was still too amped to sleep, so grabbed my computer and began journaling. What a day it had been! My first day back to Taipei, Taiwan since my adoption. I thought it entirely ironic that my adoption fell close to the New Year, just as the reunion with my birth family was taking place during the Chinese New Year. Everything was coming full circle as though it was meant to be.

After completing my journal entry, I got ready for bed and watched a little TV. I found a series, *Merlin*, in English and stayed up late watching a few episodes. Finally, I reached over to turn off the light and television. "Goodnight, 晚安, *Wǎn ān!*" Christina and Amy I whispered before falling into a restful sleep.

姐妹

Sisters

17.

You are blood. You are sisters. No man can break that bond.
~ Kim Boykin, A Peach of a Pair

I woke up around 3:30 am, unable to get back to sleep. I tossed and turned before finally flipping on the light and crawling out of bed. The previous day's events flooded my mind, and there was no use trying to fall back to sleep. I crawled back into bed and thought about my sisters and all the things we would do together during my trip. I could not believe that I was in Taiwan. Next thing I knew, it was close to 5:30 and still dark outside. The steady hum of traffic from the streets below was a constant. I made myself a strong cup of black tea and tidied my room, then sat in my pajamas at the desk situated in the corner. I pulled out the pictures Christina had given me of Ma and Pa, examining their faces. The blanks that were once their image were no longer. I realized that Christina had gone out of her way to laminate the photographs. She and Amy were both deeply intuitive and thoughtful, and this was just the kind of thing Christina would do. I still did not see much of a resemblance between my face and Ma's, but my sisters thought that I looked very much like her in her younger years. Amy had also remarked that the shape of my face resembled Uncle's. I would meet Uncle on the eve of the Chinese New Year when the family would gather together to celebrate our reunion. Christina implied that Ma and Pa had suffered greatly, especially Ma, after they fled China for Taiwan following the Chinese Civil War. Ma was separated from her own mother in China as a result of the war and unable to visit her for many years. The loss of her mother and everything familiar as well as the conflict between her and Pa must have been greatly distressing. I was infinitely curious about our family history, and although Christina had shared some of the difficult times, I yearned to know more. I sensed, however, that she was reluctant to reveal more, and I did not want to push it.

The morning sun crept out, and I drew back the curtains to see another sky full of gray clouds. I wondered if it would rain again today. To my astonishment, I did not yet feel jetlagged and was looking forward to the interviews Tien had scheduled that morning. I would be interviewed by two different reporters from two local newspapers. I wondered if I should dress casually or dressy? I looked through my closet and decided to wear a pair of jeans, a red sweater, and my black boots. I was a little nervous about meeting with the reporters and what they might ask, although Tien had sent a list of questions before the trip that I had already written replies to.

About mid-morning, Tien and her friend, Elaine, who I was originally going to pay to be my guide and interpreter, met me downstairs in the lobby before the first interview. I was happy to see Tien and to meet Elaine.

"How are you this morning, Marijane?" Tien asked brightly.

"I'm doing great! I can't believe we're here, Tien." I answered.

"Yes, it has finally happened," she replied. She introduced me to Elaine. Elaine had a pleasant face and extended her hand warmly to shake mine. Elaine would assist with interpreting during the interviews if necessary.

The first reporter arrived, a female reporter from the Taipei Times. She looked to be no older than sixteen, although I assumed her to be in her twenties. She introduced herself in fluent English, and Tien ushered us into one of the hotel restaurants for the interview. The room was divided by a brightly polished brass railing, and we sat comfortably in burgundy red seats around a small mahogany table edged with gold studs. We ordered drinks and became more acquainted before settling into the interview. The reporter handed me a long, narrow red banner with Mandarin characters wishing me a Happy New Year. It was quite unexpected. I thanked her for the gift, touched by her thoughtfulness. She was extremely polite and respectful, as if I were an elder, and I could not help but feel my age as we conversed. Once we received our drinks, she asked to record the interview and turned on her recording device after I agreed. The reporter asked several questions about my adoptive parents and how I found my sisters. Although I was excited to share my story, I felt uncomfortable with all the attention focused on me and almost robotic in my answers. My face began to ache from smiling. It all felt so unnatural.

The reporter asked one last unexpected question, "If you could think of one very special event that occurred with your parents, what would it be?"

I was tongue-tied. Her question completely threw me off guard, and I could not think of a single thing to say. There were many special events with my parents - birthdays, holidays, piano recitals, vacations - but I drew a blank. Instead I said how much I regretted not visiting my parents more often before they passed away, tears sprang from my eyes. I was overcome with a mix of emotions —sadness, regret, guilt, and embarrassment - that took me by surprise. I was uncomfortable with sharing such a vulnerable moment with a complete stranger, and Tien gave me a little pat on the back as I tried to pull myself together. I grabbed a napkin and dabbed at my eyes. At the end of the interview, the reporter asked to take a few pictures, so we headed out to the lobby. I smiled as best I could for the camera and hoped that I did not have a smear of mascara underneath my eyes.

Before the reporter finished taking pictures, the next reporter arrived. The second reporter was a slender young man from United Daily News, a well-known newspaper in Taipei. A camera hung low around his neck, and he wore a long ponytail. I noticed that his fingernails extended about a quarter of an inch from the tips of his fingers, finely filed and shaped. I wondered if that was fashionable for young men in Taiwan. The reporter did not introduce himself, but immediately turned to Tien and spoke to her in Mandarin. I felt self-conscious and keenly aware of my inability to speak Mandarin. After the reporter shot a few photos, we all returned to the restaurant, and he launched into the interview. He asked what I thought about Taiwan in Mandarin, what my plans were while here, if I would continue my relationship with my sisters, and what it meant to be reunited with them. The reporter waited patiently as Tien translated each question, and I tried to make my answers succinct. The interview felt much more formal and impersonal than the last, and I wondered if this reporter was bored. I told him that I had made a photo album for my sisters and brought gifts for the family. He asked to photograph them, so I ran to my room as quickly as I could to retrieve the album and a few gifts. Once downstairs, we found a sunny spot near a window, and I sat holding the photo album and gifts as the reporter photographed away, a smile plastered to my face. After he was satisfied with the pictures, the reporter thanked me for the interview and went about his way. My face felt like it had turned to cement.

I was relieved the interviews were over and felt my shoulders relax. Elaine and I chatted while Tien went off to make some phone calls. Elaine confessed to me that prior to the interview, she had held a very negative view of adoption.

"I think it too difficult for a mother to give up her child," Elaine said, and I agreed with her.

"I can't imagine giving up a child and all the pain it must cause," I replied and thought of Ma.

Tien rejoined us after finishing her calls and suggested I contact Christina to tell her the interviews were over. When I phoned her, Christina and Amy were already on their way to the hotel to meet us for lunch. Perfect timing. I had skipped breakfast and was starved.

As soon as my sisters arrived, we caught taxis to Sogo, a popular department store in Taipei, to have lunch. The streets were busy, and motorists zipped in and out between cars on their motorbikes. We soon approached a sizeable white building with solid red pillars. The front of the building displayed "SOGO" in giant red letters and Mandarin characters. Shoppers littered the sidewalks looking for bargain deals no doubt. Once inside, we took an elevator to the eleventh floor where there was a very large restaurant. We were led to a table and served hot green tea. Christina, Amy, Tien, and Elaine talked excitedly, and I became dizzy listening to the gentle pitch of Mandarin. I did not mind and zoned out a little while they conversed. Christina would turn to me every so often to interpret what was being said.

Once our food was ordered, it began arriving quickly in courses. There were various kinds of meats in delicious sauces, steamed vegetables, and of course, bowls of white sticky rice. One dish after another came. My sisters would occasionally lean over and add more food to my plate as it neared empty. I thought it to be a cultural practice and tried not to let it bother me. I eventually covered my plate with my hands in protest, and my sisters commented on how little I ate. I was not used to eating so much food, but did not want to be rude either. Our meal ended with dessert - a black sesame seed pudding.

"It's nutrius," Christina told me, and I smiled, knowing she meant, nutritious. I had never eaten or tasted anything like it, but savored the sweet, nutty flavor.

With lunch over, we parted ways with Tien and Elaine. My sisters wanted to take me to Longshan Temple, one of the largest and oldest temples in the historic Wanhua district. We jumped right into another taxi, my sisters excited to show me around. Longshan Temple was enormous. Hundreds of small yellow lanterns suspended in horizontal rows decorated the entrance of the temple. We walked through a colorful giant archway supported by four massive pillars. Because it was near the Lunar New Year, the temple was very crowded. People were everywhere, worshipping and taking pictures. The temple itself was stunning. The roof was inlaid with vertical rows of circular orange stones, and green stones adorned the bottom edge. Two giant red lanterns were strewn from either side of the roof, and ornate golden trim hung low from the eaves. On all four corners of the roof, a single, large dragon arose prominently, each facing towards the center. The dragons, Amy told me, offered protection. To the right, there was a waterfall, the sound of rushing water gushed, and green tropical foliage below grew abundantly. As we entered the temple, I was immediately assaulted by the smell of burning incense. I struggled to catch my breath as thick white smoke filled the air. Gold and red accented the decorative buildings and walls, and there was a large altar for worshipping as well as a long table set with fruit and dishes of food in worship of Buddha. As we reached the altar, Christina and Amy each took three sticks of incense from a cylinder, and Christina handed me three sticks. We bowed our heads and joined others in prayer - I thanked God that I had found my sisters. As we continued to walk through the temple, Christina explained its history. The temple was badly damaged during World War Two by American bombers. It was believed that the Japanese were hiding arms inside the temple, and the U.S. retaliated with heavy bombing raids. I thought of my father, who was a B-24 pilot in the U.S. Army Air Corp and had flown in the European Theatre. What a terrifying time that must have been for all. I could not fathom dropping bombs on any country, but I was especially glad that Dad had not flown over Taiwan.

Before our visit to the temple ended, my sisters and I stopped to take pictures. Christina happily maneuvered me from one spot to another in front of the temple, clicking wildly. I posed with Amy, then Christina switched places with her, and Amy took more pictures.

"Christina love taking pictures of everything!" Amy said, and we both laughed. My sisters hailed a taxi afterwards, and we headed to Christina's apartment in Banciao District, a municipality of New Taipei City. I knew very little about Taipei and believed it to be one big city; however, Taipei was divided into six different municipalities including New Taipei City.

Christina lived in a tall apartment building on an upper floor, and we took the elevator up. As soon as we stepped inside, my sisters removed their shoes, so I followed step. Christina's apartment was modern and spacious with light hardwood floors. Light shone through a sliding glass door that looked out onto the street below, a potted plant with magenta flowers sat upon an end table. I noticed a bookshelf in one area of the room stacked with books, and colorful artwork accented the walls.

"It is a good thing you arrived because it make me clean up!" Christina said.

Everything seemed neat and put in its place. Two beige sofas decorated with throw pillows, a coffee table, and television sat in the living room, and a small dining set was centered off to the corner. The kitchen was hidden behind a door, a curtain of coffee-colored beads dangled from the doorframe. I was not sure how many bedrooms there were, but did not want to snoop. Amy disappeared into the kitchen to prepare a light dinner as Christina took out a photo album. *"Holy cow, I was in the living room of my oldest sister in Taiwan!"* It still seemed so surreal. Christina sat next to me on the sofa as I looked through the photo album. She showed me wedding pictures and photos of her and Amy during their college years. I thought I resembled Amy as I gazed at the photos. We came across a random picture of Ma. She looked very much like she did in the photograph Christina gave me, except more relaxed, a slight smile upon her lips.

Awhile later, Amy brought out our meal. It was simple, warm and delicious. Christina told me that Amy did most of the cooking for her when, Michael, her husband, was away on business. We drank aromatic Mountain tea following our meal, the dark green tea leaves slowly settled to the bottom of my cup. We talked about movies and music, and Christina said that she enjoyed watching Korean dramas. One of her favorites was *City Hunter*, which happened to be one of my favorites, too. I was learning that my sisters and I had much in common! Christina then put on a Korean drama called *Sweet Spy*. There were no English subtitles, but I was able to get the gist of what was happening. Christina occasionally interpreted what the actors were saying. The language barrier was a challenge, but we were managing well, and it was pure bliss to be in the company of my sisters.

As the night wore on, the adrenaline tapered off, and I felt myself quickly fading. We had a very early morning the next day and would be traveling to Hualien, about a two-hour train ride east. My sisters accompanied me downstairs and instructed the taxi driver where to take me after handing him some money. I knew it futile to protest paying for the taxi myself, so I accepted their gesture to pay for the fare.

"Xìe xie," 谢谢, thank you, I said, giving Christina and Amy a hug. I thanked them for a wonderful day and wished them, *"Zài jiàn,"* 再见, or good night. Christina and Amy smiled at my feeble attempt to speak Mandarin. As we pulled away, the taxi driver began speaking to me in Mandarin.

I replied slowly, *"Wǒ huì shuō yì diǎnr zhōngwén,"* 我会说一点儿中文, meaning "I can speak a little Chinese." We both laughed, and the driver nodded his head and said something else I did not understand in Mandarin. We drove in silence the rest of the way. The ride back was about a half hour. The streets were dark, lit by bright lights and big neon signs advertising movies and commercials. People sat outside eating, drinking, and walking along the sidewalks. I watched the passersby and thought about my last two days in Taiwan. I could not have been happier. My sisters and I had many common interests - a love of music, the arts, and Korean dramas. Christina seemed the leader of the two, perhaps because she was the elder, but both she and Amy were strong, intelligent women with generous spirits, and I very much admired that about them. My thoughts turned to the family reunion to take place next week on the eve of Chinese New Year. I did not want my family in Taiwan to think of me as a spoiled American. My immediate family back home and I were certainly not wealthy, but had also been blessed with much. Christina expressed several times that she thought my parents to be angels and was happy I had been raised in the U.S. I hoped that I could reciprocate my sisters' generosity. Although I barely knew them, I felt a sisterly bond almost instantaneously, despite the cultural barrier. We were blood, and surely nothing could break that bond.

I woke up the next morning to the sound of my alarm clock, groggy and slightly disoriented. It was 5:30 am. My room was pitch dark. My sisters and I would be traveling to Hualien today. I stayed in bed a few minutes longer before dragging myself to the bathroom. The toilet seat warmed up quickly with the touch of a button, and I wondered if all hotels in Taiwan came equipped with electronic seat warmers. I brushed my teeth and put in my contact lenses, all the while worrying that I would get lost on the way to the MRT that morning. Christina and Amy would be waiting for me at the train station by seven to catch a train to Hualien. I dressed sluggishly then made my way downstairs with my suitcase and out of the hotel. The twilight sky gave me just enough light to follow the map Christina had drawn for me to the MRT, and I walked briskly trying to warm my body. About ten minutes later, I arrived at the station. I have a horrible sense of direction, but made it without getting lost. The station was already bustling with people waiting to catch their trains. I found Amy and Christina easily amid the crowd. Their cheery smiles made getting up so early in the morning worth it. Amy handed me a hot coffee in a small Styrofoam cup and a sweet roll wrapped in cellophane. I was not hungry, but ate the roll anyway. Amy had packed a small lunch bag full of snacks for the train ride. She wore a bright fuchsia sweatshirt and black jeans, and Christina was dressed in a tan vest zipped up over a light pink long-sleeved sweater and gray pants. They each had a small suitcase. I was amazed that neither of my sisters seemed at all tired, but appeared to have endless amounts of energy.

131

"Okay, Marijane, I think it's time," Christina said. We made our way to our train and boarded. My sisters paid for my train fare. Christina had arranged ahead of time for hotel accommodations, a driver to take us sightseeing, and for our meals in Hualien. My sisters refused to let me pay for anything. I was very grateful for their generosity, but was concerned about how much money they were spending on me. Soon, we were pulling out of the city. Tall buildings and overpasses flew past and before long, the countryside stretched out before us. The train picked up speed. I began to feel sleepy as the car rocked gently along the tracks. Amy encouraged me to sleep. I closed my eyes and tried to rest. It was not very long, however, before I needed to use the restroom. I asked Christina where the restroom was, and she pointed towards the back of the train.

"Just hold on," Christina said with a funny look on her face as I excused myself and squeezed past her and Amy. I thought it strange, as the train ride was actually very smooth. Once I made it to the restroom, I understood what she had meant. Instead of a toilet, there was a small in-ground bowl at floor level, or a squat toilet, with a silver chain for flushing. I had not seen one of those types of commodes since a college trip to China back in 1986. *"Oh geez,"* I thought. *"This will be fun."*

When we arrived in Hualien a couple of hours later, our driver, Mr. He, met us at the train station. Mr. He was an older gentleman with a warm smile and raspy voice. He wore a bright red baseball cap and T-shirt with the words, "Thailand Phuket," written around a dancing elephant, a small belly hung over his pants. Mr. He seemed pleased to load our luggage into the trunk of his car and be of service. He and my sisters greeted each other warmly, as though they had known each other a long time. We would spend the day at Taroko Gorge National Park before traveling on and lodging at our hotel along the coast.

Taiwan's natural beauty was spectacularly displayed at Taroko Gorge, and the park stretched for miles and miles, replete with hiking trails and wildlife. I learned that "Taroko" was one of sixteen aboriginal tribes in Taiwan and meant, "old, wise people." Taroko National Park, the second largest park in Taiwan sprawled across acres of lush green and teeming rainforests. The park is famous for its mountains and marble canyons. Mr. He drove us up the winding mountainside leisurely.

I was afraid that I might get carsick on the way up and had placed another patch of scopolamine behind my ear. I was relieved that the curves were mild. We reached the top about a half hour or so later. Breathtaking panoramas of the park appeared at every turn. Marble rock faces plummeted into deep chasms, crystal waterfalls fell over hillsides, and pine-covered alpines reached up towards the clear blue sky. We hiked throughout the park for several hours, stopping to take photographs at the Tunnel of Nine Turns, Swallow Grotto, Bridge of the Kind Mother, and the Eternal Springs Shrine. Taroko National Park was a photographer's dream. I shot pictures of Tar Peak Bridge, a red metal bridge that extended for miles over the gorges below and Frog Toad Rock, a rock formation that many said looked like a frog prince. A pavilion constructed on top of the rock formed a "crown" and was built by Prime Minister and later President Jiang, Jing-Guo in memory of his mother. Christina explained that many veterans lost their lives while building the expanse of cavernous archways and tunnels, and the Eternal Springs Shrine was built to commemorate them. Tourists exited tour buses along the tunnel path. I noticed signs warning guests of falling rock. We walked and walked until my legs grew tired.

After the park, we got back into Mr. He's car and travelled on, stopping for lunch at a little restaurant on the side of the road. The food was scrumptious; I was beginning to fall in love with Taiwanese food. We then continued our journey to the beach house where we would stay overnight. Christina, Amy, and Mr. He conversed in Mandarin, and I eventually dosed off, the effects of scopolamine numbing my senses. When we arrived at our beachside inn, it was completely dark outside, but I could hear the loud rumble of the ocean. I was so tired that all I wanted to do was fall into bed. The inn was just meters away from the Pacific Ocean, and my feet sank into sand as we trudged into the lobby where our hostess greeted us cordially. Christina led me up a narrow spiral staircase to my own private suite. I hastily thanked her for another remarkable day, anxious to get ready for bed. As soon as my head hit the pillow, I fell into a dreamless sleep, the crash of ocean waves bid me good night.

I was not sure what time it was. Soft light filtered in through my window and white cotton shades. My body felt heavy as I stretched and wiped the sleep from my eyes. I got up and walked slowly to the window then reached to open it. The smell of saltwater was like a gentle balm, and the sun warmed my face. It promised to be a beautiful day. I sauntered into the tiny bathroom adjacent to my bedroom and turned on the shower. I was sure a hot shower would wake me up out of the fog that obscured my thoughts. We had not set a time to meet this morning, nevertheless I sped through my morning routine just in case my sisters and Mr. He were waiting for me downstairs. My suite had a separate living area that I had barely noticed the night before with a couch and chairs, as well as complimentary coffee and teas. I made myself a cup of hot tea and lounged around for a bit before heading downstairs. Christina, Amy, and Mr. He were already there visiting with our hostess, who had prepared a generous meal. The inn reminded me of a beachside cottage. The ceilings were covered in cedar wood planks with dark beams, and several large windows faced out toward the beach. We all sat down, and my sisters encouraged me to eat. It was rare to experience such genuine hospitality. When breakfast was over, my sisters and I strolled outside to the beach. The weather was absolutely gorgeous. A balmy wind swept gently across my cheek as we walked over sand dunes toward the water's edge. We took turns with the camera making sure we had multiple shots together. Christina went back inside the inn to make sure everything was settled before we left. Amy and I stood on the beach together enjoying the sand and surf.

We would continue sightseeing on our way back to Taipei with Mr. He. Our first stop was Pine Gardens Annex, a well-preserved historic site in Hualien City that once housed Japanese command quarters during World War Two. It was said that Japanese Kamikaze pilots gathered at this site where they were given the most exquisite wine from their emperor on the eve of their suicide missions. At the end of the war, Taiwan was handed over to The People's Republic of China (ROC) following Japan's defeat, and the compound was used as a vacation resort for U.S. servicemen. As its name suggested Pine Gardens was surrounded by old, tall Okinawan pine trees brought in by the Japanese in the early 1900's. The trees were thought to be over a hundred years old. The annex sat atop a slow rising hill overlooking the beautiful Hualien harbor and mouth of the Meilun River. Inside the annex, there were quaint art and gift shops, a wishing pond covered in lily pads, and a small café. I perused the gift shops and bought Taiwanese bookmarks to bring back home to Lexie as my sisters shopped.

Mr. He drove us onward from Pine Gardens to a natural hot springs resort. I was fatigued and looked forward to soaking in a hot mineral bath. When we arrived, we were shown to three small private bathing rooms each fitted with a large bath and bench. The bath and tiles were a muddy pink and looked as though they had seen many a bather. I soaked my feet as the bath filled with hot water. After relaxing for several minutes, I dressed and headed back out. My sisters joined me shortly thereafter, their faces flushed and dewy. We ate lunch next door in the resort before hitting the road again. Mr. He took us to some local shops, including a dried beef and pork store. My sisters bought several packages of turkey and beef jerky for Pat as well as Taiwan candies and other yummy treats for Lexie.

As evening approached, Mr. He drove us to the train station. The last two days had been glorious. Although I was fatigued, my sisters encouraged me, and I cherished the time with them. I felt comfortable in their presence and greatly appreciated their desire to show me all of Taiwan. It was as though we were making up for lost time. When we arrived at the station, Mr. He unloaded our luggage, and we said our good-byes and wished him well. I thanked him for his endless hospitality and generosity. He smiled and waved as we proceeded onto the train. *"Good-bye Hualien,"* I thought as our train pulled away. Tomorrow would be another big day. My sisters and I would visit the shrine where our parents laid at eternal rest. I greatly anticipated paying my respects to my birthparents, but for now, quieted my mind as I watched Hualien slowly disappear into a golden sunset.

重聚

Reunited

18.

The sweetness of reunion is the joy of heaven.
~ Richard Paul Evans, *Lost December*

Darkness was all around. Malevolent hands clawed at my body, pinching my sides, greedy to pull me into the dark shadows. I tried frantically to free myself and scream, but no sound escaped my lips. I continued to struggle, falling through air, my body contorting. The hands mercilessly tightened their cold grip. I startled awake. It was the same nightmare that haunted me as a young girl. Sleep paralysis had plagued me, but I had not experienced it in a long while until now. I sat up in bed, pulling the covers around me, shivering, trying to orient myself. *"It was just a dream, Marijane. Shake it off."* I commanded myself out of bed to the bathroom. Every step felt leaden. It was my second week in Taiwan, and a morning I had greatly anticipated. My sisters and I planned to visit our parent's shrine and would leave early for the two-hour drive to the mountains. My excitement was dulled by a compelling sense of foreboding. *What was up with me?*

I stepped into the shower. Surely a nice, hot shower would revive me. Afterwards, however, I still felt fatigued and out of sorts. I hoped that after eating, I would feel better and noshed on a protein bar before heading downstairs to meet Christina and Amy. In my imagination, I tried to envision the shrine where my birthparents laid at rest. The word, "shrine," sounded so mysterious to me, eerie. Christina alluded previously that the shrine was built along a mountainside. Would it look like the colorful temples I had seen throughout the city? I imagined it to be a very peaceful place. I visualized a mountainside with a stone path and bold archway leading to a sacred space enshrouded by forest greens. It was no doubt a place of reverence. Ancestor veneration was an ancient, honored practice in Taiwan and China steeped in love and respect to reminisce the deeds of the dead. It stemmed from beliefs that the dead had a continued existence. I wondered, *"What would it be like to honor my birthparents at the site of their tombs?"* Ironically, I learned much later from a Taiwanese friend of ours in Arizona that many Taiwanese when they traveled to the U.S. were horrified that big, beautiful homes were built on the sides of mountains. In Taiwan, mountainsides were for the tombs of loved ones, not for multi-millionaire dollar homes.

I finished my protein bar and took the elevator downstairs to the lobby. It was a beautiful, crisp morning, and the sun shone brightly. Christina and Amy were dressed warmly and greeted me with smiles.

"Are you ready to go, Marijane?" Christina asked.

"Yes, I'm ready!" I answered. We walked outside where a taxi was awaiting us. The driver appeared good-humored and pleased to take us on our special journey. As I stepped into the taxi, a strong odor of smoke mingled with cheap air freshener assailed my senses. It made me feel queasy. I sat cocooned between Christina and Amy. The backseat was surprisingly deep and roomy, and my sisters chatted happily as the taxi slowly pulled away from the hotel. I smiled weakly.

Buildings and concrete whizzed by as we left city limits and headed towards the countryside. Majestic, snow-capped mountains loomed in the distance. With every turn of my head, the queasiness increased. I forced a smile and attempted to talk to my sisters, but feared that a full-blown episode of nausea would overtake me if I continued.

"How long is the ride to the shrine again?" I asked Christina feebly.

"Ah, it's a little ways," she replied.

"Okay. I think I need to stop talking for a bit. I'm starting to feel a little nauseous," I said trying not to sound too offensive.

"Are you okay?" Christina asked, concerned.

"Yea, I think I just need to rest," I replied. I laid my head back on the seat. The odor in the taxi became noxious. I worried that I was not going to make it to the shrine without getting sick. Christina and Amy talked quietly while I closed my eyes. The nausea only worsened. Not more than an hour into our drive, I asked my sisters if we could find a restroom.

"Yes, yes," Christina said. The taxi pulled into a gas station. As I got out of the taxi, I felt the world spinning around me and stumbled into the restroom. *"Oh great. Another squat toilet."* At least it was clean. I willed myself not to get sick, taking in slow deep breaths, relieved to be outside the confines of the taxi. *"One, two, three. Breathe in, breathe out,"* I said to myself, focusing my attention on anything but the nausea. My fingertips were tingling and started to feel numb. I walked cautiously back to the taxi.

"Christina, I don't think I can go on," I said regretfully, leaning against the taxi. "I'm feeling really sick. I don't know why. I don't know what happened. Do you think you could take me back to my hotel?" I asked. "I'm so sorry." Christina and Amy looked at me, their brows knit together in worry.

"No, no. It's no problem!" Christina quickly replied. "We turn around." They took hold of my arms and helped me into the front seat of the taxi, explaining to our driver that we needed to turn back. They continued speaking in Mandarin rapidly, and I wondered what they were saying.

The drive back was torturous. Every stop, turn, and bump jolted me further into nausea as our driver drove precariously back to the city. I leaned my seat back as far as it would go, eyes shut, the backside of one forearm resting gingerly across my forehead. I tried to stay as still as possible and quiet my mind. *"One, two, three. Breathe in, breathe out."* I felt cold and clammy, as though I might pass out, my heartbeat echoed in my ears. By the time we made it back to my hotel, I was so dizzy, I could not move. My sisters again spoke rapidly to our driver. I could hear the concern in their voices, despite my inability to understand what they were saying.

"Marijane, we think you need to go to hospital," Christina said.

"No, no!" It's okay. If you could just help me to my room," I whimpered. When I attempted to open the taxi door, however, nausea overtook me, and I slumped back against the car seat. I could not stand up. My sisters stood by the door, wondering what to do.

"Marijane, we take you to hospital," Christina said firmly. I was feeling worse by the minute and agreed reluctantly, feeling awful that I had put my sisters in such a position. The taxi driver was also concerned and drove as quickly as possible to the hospital, which was a short distance from the hotel. When we arrived, a gurney was brought to the side of the taxi. My fingers were completely numb, and I could no longer feel my legs. Cold crept through my body, and it felt as though my heart were slowing down with every beat. I feared losing consciousness and tried to focus on breathing to prevent myself from passing out. A hospital employee reached inside the taxi to pull me out and placed me on top of the gurney, strapping the belt across my waist. The white sheets of the gurney felt cool. I could hear my sisters speaking to the employee as he wheeled me inside. I was maneuvered first into one room, and a hospital band was hastily placed around my wrist. I opened my eyes weakly as I was rolled away and took in the faces of small Chinese children and strangers staring at me. I closed my eyes again. We reached another room, a much quieter space. I just wanted all movement to stop. Each time the gurney turned a corner, I felt a new, sickening wave of nausea. I kept my eyes shut knowing that Christina and Amy were close by. When the doctor finally arrived, she greeted me in English. My sisters explained to her what happened.

"Marijane, I'm sorry that you're not feeling well. We're going to take some tests, okay?" the doctor said. I nodded my head and half opened my eyes to see a thin woman wearing hospital scrubs and a white coat, her face obscured by a surgical mask. A few minutes later, a technician came to draw blood.

"Don't worry, Marijane," my sisters assured me. "This won't hurt much." I was too nauseous to care. The tech rolled up my sleeve and administered the draw. I barely felt the prick of the needle. Several minutes went by before another technician visited.

"Marijane, they give you a shot," Christina explained haltingly. "You need to turn to your side and unbutton pants." *"Oh man,"* I thought miserably. As sick as I felt, I was still slightly embarrassed. I felt the cold, wet swab of alcohol on my hip, following by a sharp pinch as the tech injected me with some unknown medication. Afterwards, I rolled back over. My sisters were standing very close, talking over me. I hoped that the nausea would subside soon and wished for sleep. Then one sister reached over to poke my hipbone. I was not sure which sister because I continued to keep my eyes closed. Did they think I was too thin? Several more minutes went by before the doctor came back with the test results.

"Your potassium level is very low. And your electrolytes are imbalanced," the doctor said. *"What does that mean?"* I thought. She prescribed rest and liquids to stay hydrated, but not much of anything else. We stayed in the room, and I rested for what seemed like a couple of hours, drifting in and out of wakefulness. When I finally awoke, my sisters were there beside me. I opened my eyes, adjusting slowly to the light. The room was tiny and white. There were no chairs for sitting. After a few minutes, Christina asked softly, "Marijane, would you like something to eat?" I had eaten nothing more than a small protein bar that morning. My stomach rumbled, and I felt hungry despite the nausea.

"Yes, that sounds really good," I replied.

"Amy will go get food for us," Christina said. I remained lying down on the gurney while Christina sat beside me. Not more than half an hour later, Amy returned with three bowls of *congee* (粥, *zhōu*), or rice porridge, in large Styrofoam bowls. The nausea had subsided, and I sat up carefully, trying to regain my equilibrium. A savory aroma arose from my bowl as I removed the lid. The sticky white rice porridge was thick, steamy and delicious, teeming with white chunks of broiled fish and vegetables. My sisters and I ate together in the hospital room. Christina and Amy sat on the edges of the gurney.

"Hmmm, this is so good. Thank you, Amy, for going out to get food," I said. The porridge was better than any medicine, like food for the soul. It became one of my favorite Taiwanese meals.

"Amy make best rice porridge," Christina said.

"I make for you one day," Amy continued. When we finished eating, I begged my sisters to allow me to pay for the medical expenses, but they would not have it.

"It's not like in U.S. where it cost so much," Christina explained. "Medical care not so expensive here in Taiwan." Back home, we once spent nearly $3,000 in emergency room expenses after I totaled my SUV. I could not imagine my sisters covering such expenses for me.

They reassured me, however, that that was not the case. My thanks to Christina and Amy seemed inadequate for all they had done. I could never repay their kindness.

We took a taxi back to my hotel that evening, I felt dazed and weak, but glad the nausea had gone. Christina and Amy escorted me upstairs, and Amy bought more porridge to store in my refrigerator for a later meal. I thanked them again, and apologized that we were unable to go to the shrine.

"It's okay," they said. "We go another time." My sisters said good-bye, urging me gently to rest and eat. It was early evening and the sun had not yet begun to set, but I crawled into bed anyway. What a bizarre day it had been. I was glad to rest quietly in bed, watching television. I wondered what had caused me to feel so ill. I had such a strong feeling that morning that something was off, like a premonition of sorts telling me that I would not make it to our parent's shrine that day. I did not share it with Christina and Amy because there was no explanation for what I felt. Nevertheless, it bothered me greatly that I was unable to make the journey to the shrine. When would I ever have that opportunity again? I hoped that my sisters were not too disappointed.

* * *

It had only been a couple of days since my untimely trip to the hospital. The Eve of the Lunar New Year arrived expectantly bringing with it the hope of new beginnings. People in Taiwan everywhere anticipated an evening full of social gatherings and merriment with family and friends. My sisters and I delayed sightseeing until I was fully recovered; however, nothing this night could prevent me from celebrating the New Year with my birth family. I felt like Maria in *The Sound of Music* when she first arrived at the Von Trapp mansion, full of expectancy and nervousness. What would this day be like? I wondered. My Uncle, my older brother, John, two sisters' husbands, Amy's sister-n-law, and nieces and nephews would join my sisters and I to ring in the New Year. The festivities would begin around 8:00 pm. Christina had made reservations at one of the fancy restaurants downstairs in my hotel for our entire family. A huge banquet would be served in observance of the Lunar New Year. It was the Year of the Black Water Dragon, a year I would never forget.

I gobbled down a couple slices of raisin bread from the loaf that Amy had given me previously. The bread was soft and spongy unlike raisin bread in the U.S. and was thickly sliced. I savored the light, sweet dough as it melted in my mouth, then bolted downstairs to take a walk around the city. A resounding boom echoed through the hotel lobby as I exited the elevator. A crowd of onlookers had gathered to watch the lion dance, a Chinese tradition meant to bring good luck. Everyone stood mesmerized as four male drummers played rhythmically, each strike of their drum sent the giant red lion into a frenzy, and the clash of cymbals rang out brightly. Silver tinsel and red and yellow fur accented the lion's oversized neck, eyes, and legs. The lion danced gracefully, weaving its way in and out of the crowd, and children craned their necks following its trail. The lion costume itself hid two dancers inside, one who controlled the head, and one who controlled its backside. It was common for the best lion dance teams all over Asia to enter competitions each year. The music was always just as important as the dancing, and competitors were scored on their ability to synchronize. I tapped my foot as the pulsating of drums resonated loudly through the room.

After several minutes, I slipped out of the lobby brushing past the spectators. It was another gray morning, and a light drizzle fell soundlessly from the sky. I pulled the hood of my coat over my head as I walked down the street to Starbucks. The smell of roasted coffee wafted through the tiny store as I walked in from out of the rain. It looked like any other Starbucks back in the States, and the menu was the same, except there was a staircase opposite the bar leading to another level. Commemorative tumblers and coffee mugs in every shape, color, and size were displayed on tables and shelves. I perused the shelves, and cappuccino machines hissed loudly as baristas frothed milk into a bubbly liquid. It was a special year, so I purchased two iconic tumblers. My favorite was a clear, tall plastic tumbler displaying an elegant red and gold dragon spiraling the circumference of the cup. It would always remind me of the Year of the Dragon, the year I reunited with my birth family. After paying for my purchases, I ambled upstairs with my passion fruit tea. There were large windows overlooking the city. I sat at a little table by the windows and sipped my hot tea, the heat from the stiff paper cup warming my fingers. I watched the rain trickle quietly down to the streets below. This day would forever be one of the most significant days in my adoption journey. I wondered how my birth family would receive me. Would they be as welcoming as Christina and Amy? Were they as curious about me as I was of them? I hoped it would be a joyous occasion for everyone. Once I finished my tea, I walked the streets of the district oblivious to the dreary weather then headed back to my hotel room. It felt like walking on air.

The day wore on, and I thought 8:00 would never arrive. The phone rang at precisely 8:00 pm. It was Christina and Amy.

"Hello, Marijane. "按 爱饿"(xīn nián kuài lè)! Happy New Year!" Christina said. "We're all here. But before you come down, we have some special things for you. I will come upstairs and meet you."

"Hi, Christina!" I replied. "Okay, I'll wait in my room." My heart leapt out of my chest. It was time! My entire birth family was waiting downstairs. Soon I heard a knock at my door. Christina was alone, dressed warmly in a silver puffer jacket and ski cap, a burgundy scarf swathed around her neck and carefully tucked beneath her jacket. Her cheeks were rosy from the cold, her smile radiant. In one hand she carried an umbrella, and in the other, an armful of gifts. It was obviously still raining outside, as tiny rain droplets had settled on the packages. Christina began handing me one gift after another.

"This is from your brother, John," she said, handing me the first of the gifts. It was a box of specialty teas from Taiwan beautifully packaged. I opened a small wine-colored jewelry box to find a silver chain necklace with a lovely pendant set with tiny stones like diamonds. Christina handed me another bag filled with Taiwan candies, apples, and tiny pink jewelry boxes, one containing a pair of hanging jade earrings and the other, a pair of gold stud lotuses. Christina saved the most special gift for last. Inside a small, narrow box embroidered in sage green contained an intricate name stamp with my Chinese name, Huang, Hsaio-Ling, 黃筱玲. She explained that it was customary for family members to have a personal hand, or signature stamp. The stamp itself was almost an inch in diameter and approximately six inches in length, a deep, marbled red, and fit perfectly in the palm of my hand. The top

145

of the stamp bore a finely carved miniature dragon, and a small round blue and white porcelain dish containing bright red ink accompanied the stamp. It was exquisite. Once again, there were no words to properly express my gratitude. I was deeply humbled by the generosity of my family and felt I did not deserve such lavish gifts. I hugged Christina, thanking her for the gifts. I carefully placed everything on the desk in my room and a nearby armchair and in one big swoop, collected the gifts I had wrapped previously for my family.

Christina and I went downstairs to join the rest of the family, my arms laden with gift bags. We stepped off the elevator, and there in the lobby stood my family - eleven members in all! Christina introduced me to everyone, one by one.

"Nice to meet you," my brother, John, said, extending his hand to shake mine. John was the eldest of we four siblings and wore a long-sleeved navy blue and green plaid shirt, a red and tan plaid scarf tucked into his blue vest. He had a round face like my sisters and also wore glasses. John was quiet most of the evening. I was not certain if he spoke or understood English well. Next, Amy introduced me to her two children, Victor and Jin Jin, who looked to be in their early twenties. Jin Jin was tiny with a sweet face and bubbly personality, and Victor was very handsome and polite. I was then introduced to Uncle, and his son and daughter, who both appeared to be in their early twenties. I met Christina and Amy's spouses and then Amy's sister-in-law. They were all so welcoming. I told each, "nice to meet you," in English and immediately wished that I knew more Mandarin.

Outside the restaurant, Caishen, better known as the god of Fortune, greeted us, his long ruby robe swept the floor. He wore a mask as white as lilies, and a stringy black beard hung from his chin above red lips lined with a smile. He held a banner wishing all a Happy Lunar Year in Mandarin characters. We stopped and took pictures with him. An air of excitement surrounded us as we headed into the restaurant.

The restaurant was full of diners celebrating the Lunar New Year, and happy chatter permeated the large banquet room. The walls were covered in light gray paneling punctuated by tall narrow mirrors. Round tables overlaid with burgundy red linens were placed prominently around the space. We were quickly shown to our table and took our seats. Michael, Christina's husband, was an affable fellow with a big smile and lively personality.

"Welcome home, Marijane!" Michael toasted several times throughout the evening, and the elders at the table were also honored. Michael enjoyed a good drink and a smoke, and we raised our glasses in celebration as he led us from one toast to the next.

Uncle was the patriarch of the family. He was a handsome man, quiet and observant with a gentle demeanor. His hair was greyed, eyes gentle, and I could see a strong physical resemblance to Pa, although the line of his jaw was softer. He smiled reassuringly as the evening continued.

After we were served drinks, I began passing out gifts to my family. They were appreciative, and I thought to myself how small the gifts were in comparison to what had been given to me. Before long, our meal was served. The courses came out, one after another in typical Chinese style. We drank and ate, and I felt as though I were floating on a cloud. By the end of dinner, I was completely stuffed.

At the end of our meal, Uncle came to sit next to me. He wanted to give a few words, and I knew that what he intended to say would be significant, a gesture to speak on behalf of my father.

"I am not sure what my brother would say now that you are back," Uncle said in halting English. "He's not here. You are part of the Huang family, and I wish to give you something." Uncle reached out to hand me a red envelope filled with New Taiwan dollars. Red envelopes, or packets (红包, *hóngbāo*) are money wrapped in red (压岁钱, *yāsuì qián*) and given to children by their parents, grandparents and others as New Year's gifts. The Chinese regard red as the symbol of energy, happiness, and good luck. Giving red envelopes is a gesture of sending well wishes and luck. The significance of red envelopes is the red paper, not the money inside. It is hoped to bring more happiness and blessing to the receiver, and is therefore, impolite to open in front of the person who gave it to you. I did not know that at the time, but intuitively did not open the red envelope until I was alone back in my hotel room.

Will you accept this gift?" Uncle continued, his voice trembled and his eyes were watery. I was overwhelmed, humbled, and did not know what to say. I reached to take the envelope, searching for the right words

147

to express my gratitude, the eyes of each of my family members upon me. I faltered.

"*Xie xie,* 再见, " Uncle, I said and gave him a big hug. I did not know what else to say. How was I to even begin to thank him? The reunion with my birth family had surpassed all my dreams. I never imagined that I would reunite with them and, furthermore, be treated with such kindness and generosity. It was beyond understanding, beyond two worlds. At that moment, there were no cultural barriers. Only love, grace, understanding, and kindness. That was all that mattered.

As the evening continued, there was more lively conversation, snapshots, and toasts. It had been a beautiful homecoming. I wanted to honor my birth family as they had honored me. I vowed to learn Mandarin and indulge myself in Taiwanese culture as much as possible. I went to sleep that evening happier than I had felt in a long time. It had been such a rich experience meeting my birth family and celebrating the Lunar New Year with them. I remembered Amy telling me that our parent's greatest wish was for our family to be reunited one day. I imagined that Ma and Pa would say, "The sweetness of reunion is the joy of heaven."

再见

Good-bye

19.

The days following the reunion with my family, my sisters and I attempted to fit in as much sightseeing as possible before my return home. I never quite regained my health following that brief illness, which prevented us from visiting some of the attractions we had hoped to see. Nevertheless, my sisters did their best to show me highlights of Taipei.

We visited Taipei 101 located in the Xinyi Shopping District, the newest area of urban Taipei. Taipei 101 is the second tallest building in the world and a mecca of high-end shopping. It houses various banks, motor, communication and financial companies, as well as consulting groups. The building reaches a dizzying height of 1,667 feet or 508 meters, and was designed to withstand typhoons and earthquakes common to Taiwan. I could barely get a picture of the entire tower because of its incredible height. The 89th floor of the structure holds an indoor observation area where visitors can take in a 360-degree panoramic view of the city, and an outdoor observation deck is located on the 91st floor. Two elevators transport visitors to the upper levels and are the fastest in the world. My sisters asked if I wanted to visit the observatory, but I promptly declined because of my awful fear of heights.

We spent our time perusing the tower's multi-level shopping mall and ate in its bustling food court, which boasted numerous eateries.

My sisters and I each had a bento box. I enjoyed tempura shrimp and vegetables and tiny balls of sticky white rice. It was almost too pretty to eat. While we sat, a giant yellow lion danced its way around the mall in celebration of the New Year, musicians following in tow. When we finished, Christina and I chased after the lion to take pictures.

We walked from one floor to the next, exploring different stores. Gargantuan sized billboards displaying Dior and Burberry designs and fragrances towered over us, glamorous models looked as though they were ready to leap off the boards. The tower's postmodern design was sharp and elegant. We stopped in several different clothing stores. I did not want to show too much interest in any one item for fear that my sisters would want to pay for it. I admired the young, pretty saleswomen who were sharply dressed and had the most stylish haircuts. In one of the gift shops, I found a pretty porcelain tea set for Tien. It was a cheery red. I wanted to thank her for all she had done to help me find my birth family. Amy agreed that the tea set would make a nice gift and refused to let me pay for it, hard as I tried. We visited a few other stores then took a taxi back to Christina's to watch movies and eat dinner. It had been another lovely day spent with my sisters.

* * *

Time seemed to fast-forward, and my return home was approaching. My sister, Amy, was preparing a special meal for Christina and me at her home the afternoon before my departure. I tried not to think about leaving the next day. I have always had a difficult time with farewells, and it left me feeling bereft to think about saying good-bye to my sisters. A weight had begun to settle right in the middle of my chest. It seemed as though I had just arrived and, here it was almost time to go. I focused on enjoying the time I had left with Christina and Amy.

That morning, my sisters took me to the Lin Family Mansion and Garden, a historical landmark in the Banciao District, New Taipei City and one of Taiwan's only remaining private gardens. In the distant past, wealthy businessmen fond of high living standards entertained government officials and business affiliates in elaborately designed mansions and gardens. Exorbitant amounts of money were often spent building such properties. War and natural decline, however, caused most Chinese-style mansions and gardens to become non-existent. The Lin Family Mansion and Garden was built around the mid 1840's. It was eventually taken over by the Japanese during their occupation of Taiwan. Years later after the Chinese Civil War, masses of people who fled China for Taiwan found refuge at the Lin Mansion. The mansion eventually fell into decline, and attempts to repair it were made throughout the years, but failed. In the late 1970's, however, the Taipei County government successfully began renovations, and the Lin Family Mansion and Garden became a top tourist attraction.

My sisters and I walked leisurely through the massive grounds stopping occasionally to take pictures. The outer walls of the buildings were covered with brick ornaments. Delicate wood and stone carvings and traditional architectural motifs representing luck and fortune embellished the doors, windows, and halls. There was also a library, a pavilion, and long, narrow bridges that arched over murky ponds. Brightly colored flowers and large trees with old, gnarly trunks and big green canopies highlighted the landscape. The beauty surrounding this historical monument was enchanting, and I was captivated by Taiwan's history and cultural heritage.

After visiting the Lin Family Mansion and Garden, we set out for Amy's home. It was a short distance, and our taxi soon pulled up to a group of white buildings that looked like apartments. My sisters and I climbed out of the taxi and, Amy led the way up a flight of stairs. We stepped inside to a tiny, modest apartment much smaller than Christina's. A pink satin sofa with small white flower blossoms and violet vines sat against one wall, and a large maple desk was situated perpendicular against another wall. In front of the sofa was a coffee table covered with a pastel striped tablecloth. Little crystal bowls filled with candies and peanuts sat atop the coffee table, and brown wooden chopsticks were laid out neatly to the side. Across the room was a television, the remote controls laid on the coffee table. There was a kitchen hidden behind a door to the left of the desk. I thought there to be perhaps two bedrooms, and there was one small bathroom that I could see.

"This is the house that Amy and I grew up in," Christina said. "You were born in another apartment not far from here. We could take you there later."

"Yes, that would be great," I replied. "I would like that." I wondered if I would have grown up in this very apartment with Amy and Christina had I not been adopted. I also wondered if I was actually born in the other house Christina referred to, or if she meant it was the home where our family lived at the time of my birth, but did not ask. Amy's family currently lived in this tiny apartment – her husband, Jin Jin, and Victor. I looked around. Amy had placed one of the landscape pictures I gave her from Arizona on a shelf. It sat displayed amongst other pictures and photographs. On top of the desk, I noticed a large computer.

"That is where I do most of my work," said Amy. She was a web designer and often traveled to Singapore and China to conduct business. Although Amy's apartment was small, it was comfortable and clean. I realized how spoiled I was growing up in America in a home probably three times the size of most apartments in Taiwan. I wondered if I could have been happy growing up with my birth family, despite all the challenges.

"Sit down, Marijane and relax!" Amy said. "I go and start lunch." Amy slipped into the kitchen to begin cooking, and Christina followed to make hot tea. Before long, Christina brought out cups of hot mountain tea in dark ceramic mugs. I waited for the tea to cool, steam curling from my mug as I held it in my hands.

Amy appeared from out of the kitchen. "Okay, lunch is ready!" she said brightly. She brought out one dish after another in pretty Chinese dishes and bowls. There was a delicious soup with tofu, mung beans, and potatoes and carrots, fat green beans with slices of pork and beef flavored with green onion, and other vegetable dishes. It was such a delicious meal. I asked Amy for her soup recipe.

"Oh, it's very simple. Just broth, vegetables, beans, and tofu. Very easy." she said. It sounded easy, but I was sure there was more to it than that. I would have to shop at the Asian market back in Arizona to buy the same kind of beans. Amy was a fantastic cook. I longed to learn how to cook like her and to use the same kind of ingredients. It was refreshing compared to the carbohydrate-laden American diet I had consumed most of my life.

Later that evening, we took a taxi to Christina's apartment. We watched a Korean drama snuggled under warm blankets on her sofa until late into the night. I reluctantly caught a taxi back to my hotel, one last time, after watching the movie with my sisters.

* * *

All too quickly, the day of my departure arrived. Had two weeks really gone by that quickly? I wiped the sleep from my eyes and sat up in bed. I still needed to pack and was grateful Christina and Amy had given me an additional suitcase to take all of the things I had accumulated back home. My flight was scheduled for late that afternoon giving me plenty of time to pack and get my things organized.

Christina and Amy picked me up early that afternoon so we could share one last meal together. Christina was wearing a salmon colored puffer jacket and matching pastel ski cap, and Amy wore her fur-collared leather jacket and a pretty mauve scarf. It was a cool, overcast day. We walked across the street to a restaurant not far from my hotel. My sisters looked at some menus briefly then ordered our food as though they had been to the restaurant before. We munched on appetizers first then ate delicious dumplings and flavorful barbecue sandwiches.

"You should take a sandwich with you to airport," Christina said.

"No, no, that's okay," I replied. I was so full after our meal, I could not imagine eating anything else the rest of the day.

My sisters gave me one last gift before we left for the airport. It was the newest CD by Taiwanese pop artist, Jay Chou. They had given me another newly released CD by Taiwanese singer/songwriter, Leehom Wang, earlier in the week. Jay Chou starred in the American film, *The Green Hornet,* just the year before. Leehom Wang was born in the U.S. and studied music at the Eastman School of Music in New York. He performed all over Asia and had a huge following in Taiwan. I enjoyed the music of both artists and had begun printing out their song lyrics in Pinyin to help me learn Mandarin. My tutor, Shuchen, was amused when I sang the songs during my Mandarin lessons. Christina also gave me three small board books like children's books to help me learn Mandarin and made a CD demonstrating how to pronounce Taiwanese Mandarin correctly.

When my sisters and I arrived at the airport, we asked a passerby to take one last picture of us together. It became one of my favorites.

We headed to one of the airport restaurants to sit and wait. Christina went to look for something in a nearby shop leaving Amy and I alone. Amy told me again that it was our parent's greatest wish for us to be reunited one day. I nodded my head. We were awestruck by all that had happened, knowing that our time together was quickly coming to an end. I told Amy that many of my friends had suggested that I write a book about our reunion.

"If you write book, I know people who could help publish in Taiwan," Amy said.

"Really?" I replied.

"Yes," Amy nodded. "I can help."

"Wow, that would be something!" I did not intend at that time to write a book, but did not dismiss the idea entirely.

Christina rejoined us, and we headed slowly to the security checkpoint. I looked at my sisters one last time.

"It has been the most wonderful time being here with you and the family! I will miss you," I said.

"Yes, we enjoy our time together very much," Christina replied, smiling. "You take care of self, Marijane. We can Skype together, and I can teach you Mandarin."

"I would like that very much," I answered. "I'll come back in a year or two." My sisters nodded in agreement.

I gave Christina and Amy each a big hug. Why were good-byes so hard?

"Please tell Uncle and the rest of our family that I said good-bye and that I was so happy to meet them," I said.

"We will. Good-bye, Marijane!" Christina and Amy waved. I waved back then turned towards security. My sisters waited until they could see me no longer before leaving.

When I boarded the plane, I could still see Christina and Amy's smiling faces in my mind. I remembered their kindness and how they looked after me with such affection. I remembered Uncle and his gentle words during our reunion. I remembered Michael's spirited toasts that made everyone laugh and how welcoming my family had been. I was leaving Taiwan a different person, richer in the sense that I had connected to a cultural heritage I once denied. My birth family had never forgotten me, and all the events leading up to our reunion had come full circle. Two weeks in Taipei with my sisters was not long enough, and yet here I was on a plane heading back to the U.S. It was hello and now suddenly good-bye, but only until we would one day meet again.

Epilogue 尾声

Upon the days and weeks following my return from Taiwan, many people stopped to ask me if I felt closure as a result of my reunion with my birth family. I thought it such an odd question. In my perspective, the reunion was a beginning as opposed to an end. Closure signified that this incredible journey was over, and I was only just beginning to learn more about my cultural roots and birth family. For months following my reunion, I sought out ways to connect to those roots most heartily – my family and I ate out at traditional Chinese restaurants frequently, and I ate rice porridge and dumplings any time I could. We found a small, Taiwanese restaurant near our home, but the food was unappetizing and nothing compared to the food I ate in Taiwan. Disappointed, we never revisited.

Soon after my return, Christina informed me that Amy's mother-in-law, the woman who was partially paralyzed and whom my sisters regarded as a mother, passed away. I was sorry to hear of their loss and that I would not have the opportunity to meet her upon my next visit. She seemed a kind woman. Months later, I learned that Christina had suffered from a pituitary adenoma and had undergone surgery in the South of Taiwan. She had not been returning my emails, and I had feared that perhaps she did not want to continue contact. However, she later wrote explaining that she had been hospitalized for several weeks. Christina thankfully recovered, although her health was greatly affected. The years piled up and before I knew it, my trip to Taiwan was in the distant past, but it continues to shine ever so brightly in my memory to this day. Many times across the years, I had planned to go back to Taiwan, but something always prevented me from returning, much to my dismay.

A couple years later, Michael, Christina's husband, arranged a trip to Las Vegas with a large group of former classmates, an excursion they planned yearly to different destinations, and Christina, Amy, and Jin Jin, Amy's daughter, were to accompany the group. Unfortunately, Michael became very sick during their travels, and he and Christina were forced to stay behind in Seattle where they were to catch their connecting flight with the group. Michael was hospitalized and underwent emergency surgery for an unbeknownst heart condition. Thankfully, he recovered before the group's trip back to Taiwan, but was weakened, and I grew worried about his health. Pat, Lexie, and I traveled to Vegas to meet Amy and Jin Jin and spent a week with them shopping, eating, and concert going. We went to see Celine Dion live in concert together. Our time with Amy and Jin Jin was precious, but all too brief, and we promised to visit Taiwan soon. During our trip to Vegas, I also met several of Michael's classmates. They were all as kind and gracious as my family. I learned in Vegas that Amy had divorced her husband, who I had met at the family reunion on the Eve of the Lunar New Year.

My sisters and I continue to stay in touch regularly via social media. Christina wrote to me last Christmas to tell me that Michael had passed away. The news was unexpected, and I was greatly saddened. I knew the family would come together to honor him and would also care for Christina after suffering such a loss. Michael had been so lively and gregarious the night I met him on the Eve of the Lunar New Year. I still envision him smiling, laughing, and making toasts. He was the type of fella that made everyone feel welcome.

I will return one day to Taiwan and take my family on my next visit. I continue to write about international adoption, race, and culture on my blog, *Beyond Two Worlds,* which has served as a platform for conversation with other adoptees and adoptive families. I also share photographs, mementos, and artifacts from my visit to Taiwan. I am frequently contacted by international adoptees who are searching for their birth families. I offer support and sometimes share their stories on my blog. Over the past few years, I have been contacted by other Taiwanese adoptees adopted from the Family Planning Association of China. We were all adopted within a few years or less of each other, and the connection I feel to them is most gratifying. To think that we may have lived in the same orphanage around the same time is staggering. The past has a way of reaching out and grabbing you in the most surprising ways. It gives me great pleasure to help adoptees with their searches or to at least provide support, especially to adoptees from Taiwan since I can offer resources that may help them with their search. I have dreams of making this passion more of a full-time endeavor.

Without a doubt, the reunion with my birth family has been one of the most significant, life-altering events of my life. I cannot imagine having never met them – it is almost unfathomable. The events that led up to my reunion were nothing short of a miracle. I believe that the interplay of destiny, faith, and persistence led to this end. And I believe that if one wishes for a connection to her birth family, it is not impossible. Call it faith or destiny or the universe pulling strings. There is something that brings it together, despite the obstacles – some spiritual force of nature that is inexplicable. I cannot imagine it any other way.

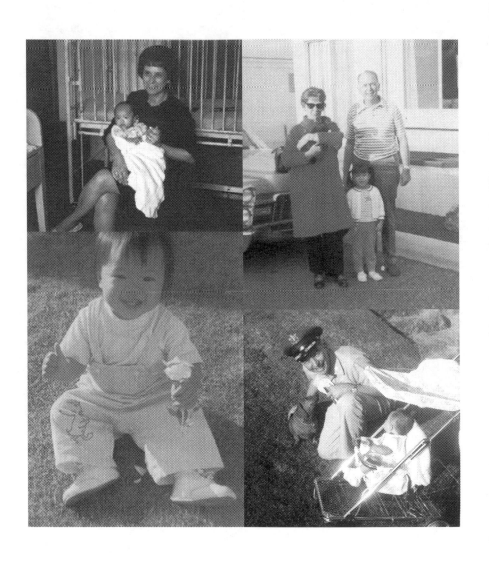

Biography 传记

Born in Taipei, Taiwan, and raised in Louisiana, USA, Marijane Huang currently lives in Long Beach, California. She is a social worker at an assisted living community specializing in memory care in another nearby beach city. She has been married for twenty-three years to her husband, Pat, and they have one daughter, Lexie, who is attending college, as well as a miniature dachshund named Peppermint. In her spare time, Marijane enjoys writing about international adoption, connecting to other adoptees, yoga, and finding new coffee shops along the coast. She also provides consultation on adoption-related concerns to adoptee groups, parent groups, professional organizations, adoption agencies, conference directors, and educational institutions. For more information on international adoption and connecting with other adoptees, please visit https://beyondtwoworlds.com.

References 参考

Bush, C.A. (1995). Healing Imagery & Music: Pathways to the Inner Self. Portland, OR: Rudra Press.

U.S. Department of State, Bureau of Consular Affairs. (2016). Intercountry Adoption Statistics, Fiscal Year 2015 Annual Report.

Verrier, N.N. (1993). The Primal Wound: Understanding the Adopted Child. Baltimore, MD: Gateway Press, Inc.

Printed in the United States
By Bookmasters